Quit Alcohol Hypnosis: Beginners Guided Self-Hypnosis & Meditations For Overcoming Alcoholism, Alcohol Anxiety, Increase Confidence, Rapid Weight Loss & Improved Health+ Deep Sleep

By Meditation Made Effortless

Copyright © 2020

All rights reserved.
No material in this book is to be utilized,
reproduced in any electronic form, including
recording, photocopying without permission
from the author.

Table of Contents

Introduction 7
Induction 9
Deepener 12
Script for Attaining Deep Relaxation 14
Script for Healing the Inner Child 19
Script for Strengthening the Immune System . 25
Script for Strengthening Motivation 29
Script for Overcoming the Compulsions 33
Script to Strengthen the Ego 40
Script for Good Health 46
Deep Cell Healing 50
Confidence and Self Esteem Script 57
Letting go of Alcohol Visualization 65
Alcohol Cessation I 73
Binge Drinking 78
Social Drinking 84
Alcohol Cessation ii 91
Alcohol Session III 95
Alcohol Session IV 98
Alcohol Session V 103

Healing the Past 117
Exploring Coping Strategies 128
Sleep Better 132
Affirmations 138

To the Narrator

The Introduction, Induction, and Deepener should be 45 Min Long
Deep Relaxation should be 20 min long
Healing the Inner Child should be 10 Min Long
Strengthening the Immune System should be 15 min long
Strengthening the Motivation should be 20 min long
Overcoming the Compulsion should be 20 min long
Strengthening the EGO should be 15 min long
Good Health should be 25 min long
Deep Cell Healing should be 20 min long
Confidence and Self Esteem should be 15 min long
Letting go of alcohol Visualisation should be 15 min long
Alcohol Cessation I should be 15min long
Binge Drinking should be 15 min long
Social Drinking should be 40 min long
Alcohol Cessation II should be 20 min long
Alcohol Cessation III should be 22 min long
Alcohol Cessation IV should be 25 min long
Alcohol Cessation V should be 40 min long
Ways to Sobriety 15 min long
Exploring Coping Strategies should be 15 min long

Sleep Better should be 25 min long
Affirmations should be 90 Min long

"…" means take a breath while speaking before you continue.

PAUSE (for a few breaths)

LONGER PAUSE (give time to allow the listener time to imagine what you've suggested)

Introduction

Thank you for choosing **Alcohol Cessation** …and choosing this audio only means, you have taken a step towards loving yourself even more.

You may have realised the cons of drinking and that is the reason you are listening to this audio. Well, congratulations on becoming aware and thinking of quitting alcohol to bring innumerable benefits to your health and relationships.

Alcohol in the past may have given you temporary pleasure but when taken in excessive quantities, it changes the chemical balance in the brain that leads to negative thoughts and emotions. It not only affects the chemicals in the brains but also directly affects the skin, pancreas, liver, and appetite.

There are many short term and long term side effects of consuming alcohol. Some of the short term effects of excessive or regular drinking are memory lapses, vision impairment, slurred speech, slowed breathing, and lack of coordination. In addition, it also affects the people around you, especially your partner and children, if you may have. It may also influence you during driving, which may result in accidents or unnecessary arguments.

You have chosen to overcome this old habit of yours, which is indeed a huge decision that will reap many benefits, in every area of your life.

This audio recording will not only reinforce the decision of quitting alcohol but also reprogram your mind to relax your mind, body, and sleep better. This will help you manage your stress better and will eliminate the craving of having a drink.

Pause

So, congratulations on taking this step of quitting alcohol for good and making a wonderful decision to better health.

Pause

I would like you to sit or lay comfortably, where you will not be distracted. Do not listen to this audio when your mind requires your conscious attention.

Pause

Listen to this audio only when you are relaxed and stationary. Please use headphones so that you can focus on the sound of my voice.

Let us start…

Begin recording

Induction

You are now listening to the sound of my voice… and the sound of my voice only …and as you continue to listen to each word I say…you allow yourself to relax more and more.

Pause

I wonder if you could take a deep breath…hold it for a count of 5… and then exhale.

Pause

Let's start now.

Breathe in Deeply…

Pause

Hold for a count of 5

1… 2…3…4…and 5

Now, exhale…
Pause

Once more, take another deep breath…

Breathe in…

Hold for a count of 5 — 1, 2, 3, 4, 5 (slowly)

Now, breathe out…
Pause

Once more, take another deep breath —

Breathe in

Hold for a count of 5 — 1, 2, 3, 4, 5 (slowly)

Now, breathe out

Pause

And, come back to your normal breathing pattern…

Pause

— And, I wonder… if you could simply bring all your focus and attention to the centre of your eyebrows…with your eyes closed…try to look at the centre of your brows and focus on the point between them…that's right.

Pause

In a moment, I am going to talk to that part of you, which is highly creative…the part that knows exactly how to help you imagine or create anything with the help of your mind's eye.

Pause

And… I know you can do it… because everybody can…we all have a creative mind, that has the ability and capability to create and imagine images in our mind.

I know you must have imagined or visualized or day-dreamed many times in your life. And… our creative part helps us imagine and visualize. Isn't it?

With the help of our creative mind, we can visualize, imagine, write, paint, and dream…and I am going to be talking to that part of you today.

Pause

Deepener

Use the power of this part of your mind to visualize yourself standing at the top of a magnificent grand staircase. This staircase has ten steps that lead to a hallway. Take a moment to look around and notice the material this staircase is made of… touch the handrails and see if the material is iron, wood, stone, or something else… The more you take note of the sight and texture of this grand staircase, the more relaxed you feel.

In a few moments, I will begin counting from 10 down to 0 and at each count, you will take a step down this magnificent grand staircase… slowly and steadily… And at each step, you will begin to feel twice as relaxed and go twice as deep…

Beginning with your right foot first, take a step down at 10… soaking in the comforts of this deep relaxation…

9… allow your body to gently drift into this beautiful state of relaxation

8… going deeper and deeper into this blissfully relaxed state of mind

7… observe this comfortable calmness settling in

6… going down further feeling more and more relaxed

5… you're halfway there

4… feel your mind and physical body relax twice as much

3… you're so close to the last step that you can see the hallway clearly

2… almost there, observe the relaxation sinking deeper and deeper

1… deeply at ease, twice as relaxed

0… you have now reached the bottom of the staircase

Longer Pause

Script for Attaining Deep Relaxation

And now, as you continue focusing on the sound of my voice and the sound of my voice only, begin to take a deep breath… Inhaling deeply and exhaling slowly and gently.

That's right.

Take another deep breath here… A gentle inhale filling up your lungs… followed by a slowly cleansing exhale.

And now as you begin to come back to a normal pace of breath… you will begin to notice all signs of tension drifting away from you and your body… The more you listen to the sound of my voice, the more at ease you become.

Continue this journey, going deeper and deeper into this beautiful state of relaxation.

Gently begin to tighten your right hand into a fist strongly as if each muscle is tensed here… and now, relax and let loose…

Pause

Repeat the same for the left hand…tightening the fist and gently loosening it… Allow both your hands to now rest loosely as if they were limp until they reach the full state of relaxation.

Now, bring all of your attention to your eyelids… Begin to squeeze them tightly and then in a moment let go of the tension in your eyelids to let them be loose and relaxed…

And now it is time to send a big wave of relaxation rolling across your entire body… beginning from the top of your head down to the tips of your toes… Let this wave bring relaxation to every nook and corner of your body.

Pause

It is time to send a second, bigger yet calmer wave of relaxation sweeping across your body from your head to your toe… Filling you up with the deepest relaxation as you continue focusing on the sound of my voice that will make you feel twice as relaxed with each passing moment…

They say the third time's a charm… Send a third wave of relaxation radiating across your body from the top of your head to the tip of your toes and see how utterly relaxed and loose all your muscles are.

Pause

There is no end to the levels of deep relaxation you can attain… As such, notice how this deep and heavy relaxation has filled up your toes, the soles of your feet, and your ankles… And how with each passing moment, this relaxation doubles in magnitude as it moves into the calves of your legs, the knees, the thighs, and the hips...

This incredible relaxation fills up your waist, your lower back, your torso, and your chest… getting magnified at each part of your body… as it continues making its way through your shoulders, your neck, the back of your neck, and your face… loosening every muscle, making you feel oh so deeply relaxed…

Feel this incredible relaxation sinking into every muscle, fiber, and bone of your body as it makes its way to your eyes, your forehead, and the top of your head… You feel so deeply relaxed as your physical body loosens and relaxes…

Pause

There is so much scope to relax even further… And now, as I begin to count down from 3 down to 1, with each count allow yourself to drift even deeper.

Beginning at 3… You can sense this relaxation everywhere in your body…

2… feel your body drifting deeper becoming even more relaxed…

1… drifting even deeper

As you continue to focus on the sound of my voice that is guiding you into this beautiful state of relaxation you feel more and more relaxed the deeper you go… and the deeper you go the more relaxed you become.

You find yourself becoming a part of a loop of relaxation, calmness, and comfort… And all you can feel within yourself are blissful feelings… As I begin counting down from 3 to 1 once again, you will find this relaxation getting magnified even further…

Pause

Starting at 3… Feeling twice as relaxed

2… drifting deeper and deeper

1… feeling more and more deeply relaxed…

As your body relaxes, your mind relaxes… And as your mind relaxes, your body relaxes even further.

You can use this method of attaining such a deep state of relaxation each time you find yourself craving any alcoholic drink.

Pause

Remember that it's a matter of diverting your thoughts from taking an alcoholic drink to indulging in productive, growth-oriented activities… And with the help of such a diversion, you will be able to attain relaxation of the mind while the thoughts of alcohol fade away.

You will have better control over your thoughts… And better control over your thoughts would mean better control over the actions that follow those thoughts.

Script for Healing the Inner Child

As you continue to vest your attention in the sound of my voice, you will slowly find yourself drifting into an incredibly beautiful state of relaxation… The more focused you are to the sound of my voice, the more serious and steadfast your resolve to quit consuming alcohol and lead a healthier and happier life becomes.

Now, upon your next inhale, you will find yourself going back in time to revisit the first time you picked up an alcoholic drink.

Pause

You can do it just like everyone else… You are going back in time to the very first time you picked up an alcoholic drink and sipped it… And as I count you down from 10 down to 0 you will find your way deeper and deeper into the subconscious mind until you arrive at the first time you sipped an alcoholic drink…

Beginning at 10…

Drifting further down into the mind at 9…

At 8 it starts to become easier to find your way across your mind…

At 7 you find yourself going even deeper…

At 6 going further deep into your subconscious mind…

At 5 you're halfway there…

At 4 you begin to see a slightly hazy picture of the memory of the first time you picked up an alcoholic drink

At 3 the haze begins to lift and the scene becomes clearer and clearer

At 2 you continue moving deeper and deeper into your subconscious mind

At 1 you are almost there and you can see the scene with more clarity

And at 0 you have reached this memory

Pause 10 seconds

And now as you begin to explore the memory of the first time you picked up an alcoholic drink, begin to zoom into this scene in your mind and explore everything and everyone around…

Was it someone else who asked you to try it or did you decide to sip alcohol all by yourself?

Just bring your attention to the reason that made you pick up the drink before moving further back in time to when you didn't consume any alcohol at all... When you were happy and stress-free...

Going further back to an even younger age... yes, just like that.

Long Pause

Maybe you are very young at this time... Look around and explore this scene... How old are you? Where are you? What are you doing?

Take an even closer look at this younger self of yours... Pay attention to the clothes you are wearing, the hair, the skin...

This younger self is your inner child... Would you love him or her just like your own child if you had one? I am sure you will... As a parent, you would give all your love to him or her unconditionally... Isn't it so?

Pause

Today is an opportunity for you to meet this child... To talk to them... Spend some time with them... To tell them how much you love them, how much they mean to you, how much you want to protect them and keep them safe and guide them at all times…

And at this moment here, you already know how wiser you are by looking at how far you've come in all these years and all that you have gone through… And with the help of all that knowledge, you will be able to guide your inner child on how to navigate through life while giving them all your wholehearted support…

Advise your inner child and motivate them with the pearls of wisdom you have…

And side by side it is time to travel forward in time together to when this younger self grows older and is about to pick up the first alcoholic drink…

Long Pause

And now you have both arrived at the time when your past self is about to pick up an alcoholic drink… Because this is a situation you have already been through before and know the ill consequences of consuming alcohol, I would like you to talk to your inner child who has accompanied you about the damaging aspects of alcohol consumption, especially on your health…

Recall here how you have promised to nurture, guide, and protect your younger self…

Keeping this in mind, what would you like to tell your past self as they are about to pick up an alcoholic drink? I would like you to share a dialogue with him or her… Tell them about the effects you have experienced when you consume alcohol… What were the ill effects of such consumption that you went through… How many times did you try to quit alcohol and how many times did you relapse? Have a heart to heart realistic conversation here…

Pause 15 seconds

Stop your past self from picking up the alcoholic drink… Stop them here because this means they will remain free of alcohol consumption all their life…

Now it's time to once again move forward in time with your younger self and arrive at present… Take a moment here to congratulate and praise your past self for listening to you…

You and your past self are a part of each other… They exist within you and you exist within them… And at this moment right here, you are together… And it is now time for your past self to integrate with you and for both of you to become one complete entity… An entity who does not consume any alcohol and stays in the pink of health for the rest of your life…

Use the power of your creative mind to imagine and visualize this integration… The two of you uniting into one… As this happens, your resolve to not consume alcohol and become healthier, joyous, and confident gets strengthened ten times over…

In unison as one entity, you are going to lead an alcohol-free, joyful, and healthy life.

That's right.

Script for Strengthening the Immune System

As you enjoy this state of deep relaxation, you allow the recording to help your inner mind in guiding your immune system to perform to the fullest. It restores your body to a vibrant state of well-being.

Pause

It is not important for us to understand and remember the functioning of the immune system to know its normal operation. We should just understand that the immune system is a product of thousands of evolutions that knows how to function normally. The conscious mind's only task is to bring the immune system back to its normal functioning.

Pause

Imagine an image of a control room in your brain that has a number of dials, switches, buttons and levers, even though there is nothing of that sort physically present in your body.

Take a look at it now.

Pause

As you look at the control room, you see a large computer in the center of the room which is the master controller of the immune system.

As you look at the screen, you notice quadrants being illustrated on it that tell you the mistakes the immune system can make. One of the quadrants is shining red to indicate that the immune system is either over-reacting or under-reacting. You will also notice a black dot in the shining quadrant that indicates how much the immune system is out of balance.

Pause

You notice a button on the keyboard that switches off the autopilot mode of the immune system, and you to switch off the autopilot mode now. Now your immune system is finding balance automatically and is normalising and returning to harmony with all the wisdom built in through evolution the endocrine glands are controlled by a set of levers next to the immune system computer.

Pause

As the immune system was out of balance, the endocrine glands have also lost their balance.

Starting with the pineal gland, you move the lever up and down to bring it to the centre position which tends the pineal gland to produce some normal hormones. As the pineal gland secretes normal hormones, imagine the gland producing some golden drops that are flowing through the body and making every part of the body harmonious and healthy. As you scan the control room, if you notice any red flashing signals, they indicate that some part of the body is not functioning properly.

Pause

You set the controllers of these body parts that are not functioning properly to the centre position so that they start functioning normally. As you set the controllers correctly, the red lights go off and green lights turn on indicating the proper functioning of the body. And now, you command your subconscious mind to automate all the positive changes that you have made today, and you switch on the autopilot mode back. gland by gland you set the controllers of all the glands right.

Pause

The pituitary gland, thyroid gland, the liver, adrenal gland, all are now producing healthy hormones and enzymes that make the functioning of your body normal. And as you set the controller of the endocrine gland back to normal, all the functions of the body become natural and normal.

Pause

Now you set your powerful inner mind to go where it needs to go to magnify each and every positive idea a hundred times over to accelerate the healing a hundred times better. Every time you take a relaxation break or listen to this recording, your mind magnifies and allows the immune system to work normally and properly. It is ideal to take a relaxation break at least once daily for 25 to 30 minutes.

Pause

Every time you meditate, pray, or relax, your immune system rejuvenates. As by taking relaxation breaks and meditating, your immune system works properly you feel emotionally, physically, and mentally stable and healthier.

Now ask your conscious mind to think about nature, or something that makes you feel comfortable and relaxed.

Script for Strengthening Motivation

By having lived and experienced the awesome life free from alcohol, you feel that you are now more motivated than ever... You feel upbeat and want to live this life every day... Each day feeling even better than the day before... Feeling healthier... Like the best version of yourself... You notice how you are glowing with the abundance of energy and vitality... Feeling incredible about yourself.

Walking along the road of the triumph of being free from all alcohol consumption, try and sense this new self of yours... How does it feel to have come so long past the critical crossroads of your life...

I want you to imagine your future self... A successful and sober you... feeling so proud of yourself... Praising yourself for your consistency and sincerity.

Pause

This road that you're one... This road of triumph... Look around and notice how beautiful it is... Look at all the lovely flowers waving the in the breeze and the lush green moist grass… The clear blue skies and the fresh air.

Bring your attention to the wonders of an alcohol-free life… Notice how confident and strong you've become as you continue feeling great about yourself.

Think about all the money you have saved by not consuming any alcohol… There is so much you can do with all that money… Perhaps buy yourself a new outfit… Or something to decorate your house… Maybe save up for a long due holiday… The possibilities are endless because of all the money you have saved day in and day out… These cumulative savings have opened so many options for you…

Pause

It is immaterial what you decide to do with all this money because you deserve to treat yourself with something special just for yourself… because you are so special… Notice how proud of yourself you are.

Long Pause

Look at the amazing human being you have become… You are dependable as you keep your word… You are diligent and consistent… You meant what you said when you quit alcohol entirely... And look how you've stood by it stoically.

Look at how far you have come... I wonder if you can go back for a moment to the time when you were still consuming alcohol... Imagine all the toxic people who surrounded you... Perhaps a friend who offers you a drink...

Pause

You can see how they are proceeding towards you with a bottle or can full of alcohol... How they are undoing the cap or cork and tilting the bottle or can in your direction...

And as this scene unravels... You begin to realize more and more how this person is not a friend at all... because a real friend helps you steer away from temptations instead of throwing them at you... A real friend helps you stick to your goals and stay determined to abstain from alcohol.

Pause

Can you hear yourself saying "No" to alcohol and mean it? Can you realize the power of your body and your mind discarding the alcohol? Now that you are aware of how alcohol is nothing but poison to your system... You don't want it... And as a result, you won't have it.

Long Pause

The moment you say "No" to alcohol, something incredible happens… You begin to experience this wonderful feeling of confidence, strength, and pride flowing through you… Filling you with an awesome sense of achievement.

Notice how fresh and strong you feel as you say "No" to alcohol and mean it… You outright deny the offer because you no longer consume alcohol now… And that is exactly how you want to be.

Every single day you feel lighter, healthier, and more joyful… You are full of confidence… You feel so much better because you no longer take alcohol…

Pause

And this feeling gets stronger… Your determination and motivation are strengthened… This makes you feel happier, fitter, and so much better than ever before…

And now that you are sober, you prefer to stay this way forever because this is so important for you… And with each passing day, all these suggestions are going to grow stronger, becoming more and more profound and powerful.

Script for Overcoming the Compulsions

As you continue to focus on the sound of my voice and the sound of my voice only, you begin to go deeper and deeper into a beautifully relaxed state of mind where you become more and more attentive to everything I say.

The more you relax, the prouder you feel about making such a positive change in your life… This change is going to bring so much confidence and great health into your life to make it all the more fulfilling.

With each word I say, you begin to feel more strongly resolute to welcome health and discard alcohol… Each time you listen to this audio, you will find your determination to stay off alcohol becoming a 1000 times stronger… You find reprieve from this gross habit… Each molecule of your being enjoys being healthy and more functional.

Pause

Your liver, your heart, your kidneys, your brain… Every single organ within you is thanking you for having made such an important decision.

You have so much more control over your choices… You feel proud and celebratory for making this decision.

There is a part of you perhaps who thought of having a drink… And there's a part of you who wants to live a healthy, alcohol-free life.

Pause

This part of you that wants to stay healthy is the part that you have become the closest of friends with… This part of you helps keep your focus on the lifelong goal of abstaining from alcohol consumption always… You are not going to give in to any temptations to become slaves of the same old habit ever again… Notice how incredibly wonderful it feels to be free and in charge.

You have complete control over your behaviours and your decisions… You have chosen this healthier, longer, and more joyous life that entails more awareness and alertness, fitness, strength, healthy mind, body, and soul, fresher breath, toxin-free body… There is no stench of alcohol in your breath and no drowsiness in your eyes.

With a fresher breath and a radiant appearance, you are more attractive to your friends, your partner, and your family.

Pause

Notice how coherent and well-balanced your thoughts are… How cleaner your mouth is… How stable your body movements are… How lighter your head is… How healthy your gut and liver is…

You are free from alcohol in every way… You have a healthier and happier life… You are sober for the entirety of your long and healthy life… No amount of stress or temptation can make you consume any alcohol anymore… You have healthier ways to cope with stress which keeps your body and mind free from harm.

When you stood at the end of two diverged paths, you could see one that led to the path of a non-alcoholic, stress-free, healthier, and happier life… You also saw the other path leading to alcohol consumption and all its ill-effects.

Pause

And every bit of your being came together to help you walk the alcohol-free path… The path that you have taken and will always take is the one that leads to a happier and healthier life, free from alcohol…

Pause

Every time you encounter the slightest thought of alcohol, you reject it outright… You are reminded of the path that you have chosen, an alcohol-free life… It reinforces that you have made this choice and you are responsible for walking on it… This fills you with more confidence, making you feel more determined to bring about positive changes to your life.

Pause

If you happen to be around any alcoholics, you feel like you have never had a drink at all… And the stench of alcohol in the air that prompts you to reject alcohol is 1000 times stronger… You are filled with a sense of pride and confidence each time you reject an alcoholic beverage or even the thought of it… You gain more and more respect for yourself which in turn makes you feel more courageous.

Pause

You are also reminded of all the money you have wasted in the past on alcohol… And how you can save more money now with this impeccable decision… Perhaps put that money to good use… Investing it in better and more productive experiences or things… Perhaps to learn something new, to improve your fitness with a gym membership, maybe save up for a big holiday… There are endless possibilities.

Pause

All this, because you have made the choice to abstain from alcohol consumption and that is the new truth of your life which is embedded in the deepest part of your being to guide you as you navigate this brand new life as a non-alcoholic.

Long Pause

The truth remains that you are a non-alcoholic… You keep hearing your mind say it to you every now and then… You may hear, "I love being free from alcohol", "I am sober for life", "I choose to be sober", "I reject alcohol", "I think and feel sober"… Though iterations may vary, the meaning remains the same…

This new truth is safely locked into the depths of your subconscious mind… This makes it your reality as you continue living in this world with this truth.

Pause

Another new truth is, "I have NO desire to consume alcohol. I completely reject alcohol consciously and subconsciously."

And this truth too goes further down into the deepest part of your mind and becomes your new reality.

Another truth is that alcohol is a thing of the past… You have left alcohol way behind in an inaccessible part of your past which holds all the ill-effects of alcohol… In the here and now, you are sober.

Pause

The truth now is, "I have moved on from my past. Alcohol is a thing of the past."

The next truth is, "I am a non-alcoholic. I am forever free from alcohol consumption."

And as these truths sink deeper into the depths of your subconscious mind, you feel confident, wise, and empowered.

Pause

You are a non-alcoholic… You have no desire to consume any alcohol… Alcohol is a thing of the past… You are free from the consumption of alcohol… You are absolutely in love and awe of your healthy body.

These new truths have locked themselves in your subconscious mind… You hear them echoing at the back of your mind like a melodious symphony… Each time you hear this truth, your determination grows stronger and more profound… Your resolution becomes unshakeable… This is your new reality… You choose to stay sober for life… Continuing to live happily and healthily.

As I begin counting from 5 down to 1, these truths will sink further deep into your subconscious mind.

Pause

Script to Strengthen the Ego

As you proceed to focus your attention on the sound of my voice, you begin to allow yourself to become more and more receptive as you go deeper into this relaxed state of mind.

You have made the resolve and you're completely ready to bring about important changes to your body… To make your life healthier and happier.

Pause

The more you listen to every word I say, the more aware you become of the times in the past when you felt proud and confident about yourself… Such a time could be in your teenage years or perhaps your adulthood…

Begin to recall that time now.

And as you call to mind those scenes and situations… I wonder if you can pick one such situation where you felt absolutely amazing, confident, happy, and had faith in your worth.

Long Pause

Now that you have chosen the said incident… It is time to watch it with your mind's eye… Start watching it from the very beginning where it started.

What did you do? How did it make you feel? What did you think about yourself?

As you become more aware of the answers to these questions as you watch this incident… Notice all the positive emotions rushing through you as you soak in the delight of this memory…

Long Pause

As you draw near the end of the incident, it is time to watch the same incident once more, but this time on a big television screen… Or an even bigger projector screen… In high definition… While you sit on a comfortable couch with the remote control in your hand…

I wonder if you can visualize this great incident playing on such a big screen… in all its glory… This incident which made you feel so amazing about yourself, so proud of yourself… So happy and confident about yourself.

As this incident starts to play, you increase the volume to full…

That's right.

As this incident continues to play on this big screen in high definition and full volume… You come to the exact moment which instilled in you the maximum confidence and joy.

And as this moment starts to play… You zoom in the scene ten times over to watch it closely in all its glory…

That's right.

Pause

You can use the remote control to make the colors more vivid in ultra-high definition.

This incident is now loud, crystal clear, and vividly defined.

I wonder if you can take a mental picture of this scene right here and store it for safekeeping somewhere in your mind.

Find a suitable place in your mind to store this picture.

Long Pause

I want you to know that you will always remember the location of this picture in your mind… And each time you begin to feel low, you can simply use this picture to remind yourself about all the courage, confidence, and joy that resides within you… You achieved it once, you can achieve it again… Use this picture as a source of empowerment.

Long Pause

I wonder if you can make it a habit of practicing to fill yourself up with this a special color of confidence each morning when you wake up… To have an amazing start to your day that sticks with you throughout.

Imagine what this color of confidence might be… A color that is special and resonates with you.

Pause

Now that you have your special color of confidence… Allow it to steadily fill you up… Moving into every nook and corner of your body… Filling up every cell, muscle, fiber, and bone.

Fill up every part of your being with this color of confidence… Which makes you feel joyful, positive, and full of energy.

With such confidence, high energy, and joy you can achieve your ideal goal weight… It becomes so much easier when you vest your faith in yourself and have high self-esteem and recognition of your self-worth.

Pause

You are well aware by now that you have been confident before… This makes you feel more confident now… And the more you practice filling yourself with this color of confidence each morning, the stronger your confidence will become.

This confidence helps you have a stronghold on your eating habits and lifestyle… It helps you lose weight by eating right and getting enough exercise regularly to burn off the extra calories.

With each passing day, your confidence grows in magnitude and strength… Your self-esteem and self-worth get magnified too… Making it easier for you to achieve your ideal goal weight.

You exude this confidence and it shows in your body language… The way you walk and the way you talk… Your friends and family are amazed to see this transformation.

Long Pause

Allow yourself to let go completely of all the fears, inhibitions, and negative emotions as they serve you no purpose… Allow yourself to feel only positive emotions like security, joy, satisfaction, confidence, and freedom.

Pause

You are well-balanced at all times… Always being mindful and living fully in the moment as you work to achieve your goals each day… Beautifully and constructively.

Long Pause

You stay cool and relaxed at all times… Focused and present… Feeling confident and secure.

Pause

Script for Good Health

I wonder if you can imagine being surrounded by a serene white light which is bright and warm… A light that is soothing and healing… You are completely safe in this light.

As you find comfort in this light, it begins to move into your body, filling it up slowly and steadily… Perhaps starting from the top of your head… Moving down towards your toes… Filling up every cell, muscle, fiber, and bone.

Pause

As this light fills your body slowly, imagine having small taps on your palms and the soles of your feet… Open these taps to allow all the negativity to flow out of your system… Creating more and more space for this white healing light to fill.

Imagine all the negativity to be like a thick, viscous, black substance… Feel the pressure it exerts as it oozes out of your system… Take note of the soothing sensation of the white light filling up the space it creates.

This dark viscous substance is made up of all your fears, sickness, and negativity… Feel the light pushing it all out of your system as it makes it way deeper and deeper down into your body.

Pause

As this light fills up every inch of your system moving from your head to your face, ears, neck, shoulders, chest, and arms… Filling you up slowly with warmth and positivity… Drawing out all the negativity and healing every cell, muscle, organ, and bone.

As this white light begins to slowly move further and further down your body, it continues to fill every inch your body with nourishment and energy.

Take note of how it heals your body as it makes its way down into your abdomen, waist, thighs, knees, calves, ankles, feet, and toes.

Allow yourself to accept this white, healing light more and more as it continues to fill every part of your being… It brings nourishment, protection, love, and care to every inch of your body inside-out.

Long pause

Pause for a moment here to do a quick, mindful body scan… See if there are any spots where this light may not have reached… See if there are any spots that still house that black viscous negativity… If there are such spots, know that it's okay… bring your focus and attention to these spots and send a blast of white light to expel every last bit of the negativity from your body.

Feel the white light driving out the black viscous negativity until there is nothing but this white healing light.

That's right.

Long Pause

Now that your body is full to the brim with this loving, healing nourishment and positive energy… It is time to close the taps you had opened earlier… Keep all this goodness intact as it gets magnified and concentrated within your body.

Take a moment here to soak in this new sense of joy and good health… Take in the feeling of what it's like to be free of all disease and discomfort.

Long Pause

From this moment on, sickness neither has a name nor a home… It is no longer a welcomed guest… It is no longer acceptable.

From this moment on, you are healthy, happy, and completely healed… You feel like a healthy person… You see yourself as a healthy person…

You have rid yourself completely of fear, sickness, negativity, and discomfort... You are loved, protected, and strong... You have reclaimed your mind, body, and soul.

From this moment on, you make positive decisions that aid the wellbeing of your mind, body, and soul... You live a healthy and fulfilling life... You attain a positive outlook in every aspect of your life to help you lead a long, healthy, and joyful life.

Deep Cell Healing

Now take a deep breath for 4, hold it for 2 seconds, and exhale slowly. . Just say "breathing in" as you are inhaling. While exhaling, say "breathing out." Repeat this cycle of breathing 6 times while you concentrate on your breathing.

That's right.

Breathe In…….Breathe Out

Another deep breath

Inhale deeply from your nose and ….exhale from your mouth.

Let's take another deep breath…

Deeply in from your nose…and out from your mouth

That's right…

Breathe in deeply…….and breathe out from your mouth now.

Take another deep breath....breathe in from your nose and breathe out from your mouth.
Perfect.

Next, I want you to bring your attention on how your feet feel, and begin to picture a thick, white sand covering every aspect of your feet and toes, the bones of your feet, the joints in your ankles, between your toes, under the nails.

Pause

And as you begin to notice or visualise the white sand on and around your feet...I would like you to remove any discomfort that you may feel in your feet and toes, and let it soak in the sand. Make sure you get rid of every last bit of tension.

Pause

Whenever the feet are pain-free and totally comfortable, imagine opening the double doors at the bottom of the feet and let the sand float out slowly, taking all the discomfort with it.

Pause

Fill in the clean white sand in your lower legs, knees and thighs and feel the tension soaking into the sand as your legs become more comfortable and heavier. Open the doors beyond your knees and let the sand slowly drift out, bringing any tension with it.

Now push the sand up the mid-section of your body, engulfing your hips and buttocks. Our buttocks are the toughest muscles in our body and retain a great deal of tension so make sure that you spend some time here feeling each muscle fibre as it relaxes and lets go of stress and tightness.

Pause

When you feel heavy and deeply rooted to the ground in this place, imagining opening the gates on your hips and let the sand go.

Pause

With this cleaning sand, gently fill your lower back, stomach area, digestive organs, hands, lungs, ribs, arms, upper back and shoulders. Starting from your lower back, feel the relief of each vertebrae of your spine, stretch out to your shoulders and focus on dissolving any knots of tension that you might have in this region. Be sure that the sand dissolves any stress inside your bones that you can sense. Open your lower back gate, and let go of all the sand.

Pause

Relax and let go of any stress or tension your stomach area, feel any contaminants and stress that you may be holding in this region. Let go of any pain or tension. Little by little, you feel your chest becoming more and more relaxed.

Enable your back, lower jaw, face and head to fill up with the sand. Pay careful attention to the back of the neck where friction knots can be found, feel these melt away into the sand. That's right.

Pause

The head and the neck feel heavy; the shoulders relax and sink down. Feel the tension behind your head, and the sand go from the forehead. Then open the doors at the back of the head and let the sand drain away into the ground, and any stress you retained in this place. Now fill your body with a perfect, pure white light, from the tip of your toes to the top of your head. Your mind is now at peace.

Imagine this bright light bathing every cell in your feet; imagine it penetrating your cells, filling the cells with love and light.

Shift this energy up to your legs and let your cells fill up with this energizing healing and love. Picture each cell's structure getting stronger and stronger.

Emphasis on the knee cells and the hip joints. Feel the bright light infuse every cell, replacing any damaged cells. Note how big every cell is. See building up of the bone cells and restoring healthy bone tissue. Enable any stress to rise and break away in those places, flowing out of your body.

Pause

Run the soothing light up gradually to fill your body's trunk. Feel the light in your stomach, intestines, pancreas, kidneys, lungs, neck, ribs, spine, back muscles, and shoulder blades, soaking into every bone. Pay particular attention to any area that may be of interest to you.

Pause

Picture your spine's cells; see each cell sparkling with power and lustre. Feel your spine become stronger and stronger. Giving you all the support, love, and care.

With this energizing light fill up each of your nerve fibres. Take the stress out of your muscles and let it melt away. The nerves are good and work well.

Put the light up to fill your head, face and arms. Picture the cells getting stronger and stronger in this area; see how quickly the DNA structure repairs. See each of the cell multiplying healthily and perfectly. Your body is strong and good, and your cells are safe and powerful.

Repeat the following affirmations:

I am perfect (7 seconds pause)

My body's cells multiply healthily, in a healthy manner. (7 seconds pause)

My organs are solid, and stable. (7 seconds pause)

Every cell in my body is a perfect expression of safety. (7 seconds pause)
All the cells inside my body function in complete harmony with each other. (7 seconds pause)

Each cell inside my body works fine. (7 seconds pause)

Cells inside my body are quickly and rapidly repairing themselves. (7 seconds pause)

Each cell in my body is lovingly enclosed. My body is strong, fluid and full of energy. I have bones which are solid and stable. I love my body, and respect it. (7 seconds pause)

I listen to my body, and take care of its needs. (7 seconds pause)

I treat my body with the respect which it deserves. Let me relax and unwind my body. Cells in my body are multiplying well. (7 seconds pause)

Every day I give positive energy to every cell in my body. (7 seconds pause)

I am so thankful to my body cells for keeping me strong and safe. (7 seconds pause)

Please take a moment to feel gratitude and happiness for your wonderful life and the unceasing wonders it brings.

Confidence and Self Esteem Script

Your mind will enter a relaxed state of mind and you will become more receptive to my suggestions.

Pause

Your subconscious mind will become receptive to new changes, changes that can potentially change your life forever.

Pause

The aim is to provide you with a happier and productive life ahead. You will soon be free from the thoughts which were limiting you from being free.

Pause

Low self-esteem and low self-confidence have their roots mostly in childhood. The reasons vary from person to person. Maybe the person suffering from the above might have had a tough childhood or unfulfilled relationships.

Pause

The words said by people in childhood have somehow hurt the fragile and healthy emotional side of the human being and this has given birth to the deep-rooted issues. But the time has finally come to change the course of your life and your subconscious mind will do the work for you today.

Pause

It will scout for the old memories in your mind and filter out the unnecessary programs which have hurt you in the past. The aim is to erase those memories and give you a new perspective on life.

We all realize at some point in our life that we should have known what was about to happen to us at some point in the past and regret not knowing the consequences beforehand. It is impossible to know normally but hypnosis can reveal those unknown facts.

Pause

This is because in hypnosis, all our levels of our mind are activated and both the conscious and subconscious mind communicate seamlessly.

Pause

Without your realization, your subconscious mind is working on the background and filtering out the events which are regarded as obstacles. In simple words, the cleaning process or the removal of junk is going on in the background. All the misconceptions, false beliefs, and negative thoughts are pulled out from the deepest corners of your mind and thrown away. This is where the younger version of your mind is telling you what you could have known back then.

Pause

Your grown-up version is convincing the younger version of your mind with positive thoughts. Thoughts such as you never wanted to hurt anyone and only spread happiness and love among the people surrounding you.

Pause

The younger version is leaving no stones unturned to convince the grown-up version that you are talented and intelligent in your way and there is no place for doubts.

All your past doubts and fear you developed back in your childhood are now neutralized. Your negative thoughts are replaced with positive thoughts. Truth is the ultimate answer you were looking for and now you got it.

Pause

No matter what the others had to say about you, the truth can never be changed. You have evolved to be a new person with a fresh mind.

Now imagine you have become the younger version of yourself.

As a child, go back to the time when you were secure and safe with your thoughts. Now come back to the present phase. You will realize that it would have been nice if you knew already what you know now. Convince the child version that everything needs not to be bad and love is prevailing in life. Praise that child and bring out the happiness from within.

Pause

Now it is time to think about the facts you wish you knew back then. Tell your child version those things you know now and convince her to remember those facts always.

Repeat if required but convince her fully about the facts and make her accept them fully. All your past doubts are now replaced with new positive thoughts. The child will now grow up to be confident and a woman with high self-esteem.

When you are done convincing, just say in your mind 'I'm done'. The time taken to perform this act of convincing may vary from a minute to a few minutes.

Pause – 30 seconds

Wait for the response from the child and then proceed. Ask your child version how it feels now.

Remember that all the changes in the child version are the changes that are happening to you today.

These thoughts, the positive ones are channeling in and out of yourself and is modeling the child version at every level. As the child changes with time, you too change, because you both are the same entity. The child is your past, your present, and your future. By simply changing her, you can change yourself completely.

Pause

Finally, today you have made the child version feel better than ever. It has now become confident and has developed a good sense of self-esteem in himself. As a result, your present self feels confident and has developed great self-esteem. Thus, hypnosis has played its part in recovering you.

Pause

Your past self has been dwelling in the old and outdated programs. Outdated programs were full of negative emotions that needed to be removed for your good.

Pause

Your work and performance today were top-notch and now you deserve to rest. The subconscious mind needs to process new information to replace the old information.

Pause

Now you possess every ability which you needed to do whatever you want in this world. Speaking of intelligence, confidence, diligence, and emotional stability, you have it all now. Your gender, height, eye color, and hair color are perfect for you and you have everything to become successful in the future.

Pause

You have changed yourself to be the better version of yourself. You have grown stronger both physically and emotionally. Now you can create a new life full of happiness and success.

There is nothing that can hold you back now.

Pause

The old programs installed in your head were the root causes of your fear and delusion. All of those have now been removed and new programs have been installed.

Pause

You will now have a new perspective on life and you will see the good side of things from now on. Thanks to your subconscious mind, all the junk has been disposed of properly and now you are free from the bindings. You will be emerging out from hypnosis now and all the new information will be stored in your memory. This session has been a successful one and always remember that once you have gained wisdom, you can never lose it.

Pause

You have emerged to be a new self and all you need to do is explore yourself for more positivity and confidence along the way. You have become intelligent and the best version of yourself.

Letting go of Alcohol Visualization

As we know, concentration is the secret of strength.

As you maintain holding your consciousness on your breathing cycle, start to imagine yourself breathing in a shining, golden, bright light.

Pause

Create a picture that this bright, radiant light is filling up all parts and cells of your body. Now the energy of your body is climbing to a new level. You can feel the positive energy throughout the body.

Pause

You can feel the sensations through your fingertips as the golden light is escaping from it and the energy is wrapping itself around the body.

Immerse yourself in the bubble of golden, bright light. At present, you are on cloud floating in your golden bubble. Your body feels comfortable, warm, and sheltered in all manner of ways. You feel protected here from all the distractions.

Pause

As you continue to float in the golden bubble, more passionate, calm, and compose you become. Let us go back to concentrating on your breathing cycle, establish the same rhythm. Now with every inhalation say" I'm light, I'm love". Try to hold your breath for a few seconds and again while exhalation repeats" I'm light, I'm love.

Pause

Count till 1 to 4 and mention "I'm light" twice and I'm love" twice.
Hold your breath for 2 counts. Then exhale for the count of 4. Again say "I'm light" twice and "I'm love" twice.

Pause

Imagine yourself rolling in a deep state of peacefulness and relaxation. Everything around you is in silence, smooth and still. You are completely feeling enduring, carefree, relaxed.

Pause

Keep enjoying these minutes, of peace and internal quietness. When negative thoughts start arising in your mind, just let them go away and come back to the attention to your breath. Concentrate on your breathing cycle and a positive attitude.

Now as you maintain this breathing cycle, keep taking deep breaths, visualize yourself breathing in a positive, curing, light which is expanding in your lungs. Your lungs are expanding with this light, fill it with positivity. Inhale liveliness in your lungs. Stuff all your body with this bright light.

Pause

Let's go to a beer garden with your buddies. Imagine you are sitting there laughing, amusing, and entertaining yourself. You are completely enjoying the company of your friends. Two of your friends are Alcoholics in that group; they start drinking in front of you and offer you a drink.

Pause

Surprisingly, you will react by saying "NO Thank you, I don't drink anymore". Your friends will be stunned by your reaction and will congratulate you for the period you are off the alcohol. They will tell you the difference between your health now and then. Your health has improved a lot; you look like a new person.

Regardless you are away from the company who drink but you can somewhat smell the drink, and it concerns and attracts you. But you are so strong mentally, inclined, and motivated towards your goal that you will never think about drinking again. Your mind knows that it is not attracted to drinking. It is without the thoughts of drinking Alcohol.

Pause

While looking at your friend who is drinking you remember your days of old how your hair and clothes used to get a whiff. But now you are enjoying your surroundings, inhale the enjoyable smell of fruity, fresh smell of your shampoo. Smell the incense of your favorite perfume on your wrist and clothes.

Pause

Let us go back to your consciousness to your lungs. Keep breathing and concentrating now each time you are breathing visualize that you are inhaling heavenly, bright white light into your lungs. White color is the relieving color for your lungs. Now you are filling your liver with this positive white light. You can feel this light entering the tissues of your liver, fill it. While this light is permeable to the liver and each cell is becoming stronger and stronger.

Pause

At this moment in time, the white light is rotating in your lungs; it is not just giving positive vibes but also clearing away all the negativity and toxins.

Pause

Carry on with the breathing deeply, inhale the white light of positivity, and keep exhaling the toxins, stress, tension out of your body. Keep saying this to your mind "My liver is healing, my liver is healthy, my liver is healing, my liver is healthy. This determination will lead you to the aim of quitting drinking.

Pause

Now the scenario is that you can easily appreciate the condition of your liver when you were drinking and now when you have quit drinking. Your liver has started to change color, it is turning light pink, fleshy color. And you know pink is the color of healthy tissues.

Pause

Assume your liver as a baby, pale pink which is healthy, well built, and powerful. It can perform all its functions properly. The cells of your tissues are consistently renewing and restoring their cells to enhance its function as a baby liver you used to have.

Pause

Look at yourself you are a completely changed healthy person you wanted to be. Witness the transformation of your lungs how healthy and strong they are looking. Your lungs are well-pleased as they look pink and moist, they are healthy.

Now with such positive vibes in your mind encircle the liver, skin, and other organs with the golden, shiny light. This light will protect your body forever. It will act as a shield to protect you from all sides.

Pause

Repeat these suggestions after me:

I am entirely in charge of my life. (5 seconds pause)

I am self-controlled and have strong determination for my aim. (5 seconds pause)

As I am not an alcoholic anymore my body is at liberty to go back to its healthy state. (5 seconds pause)

I am not compulsive towards drinking anymore. (5 seconds pause)

My body is now healthier and fit as each day passes. (5 seconds pause)

I consider my body as a temple and I choose to respect it. (5 seconds pause)

I am confidently and peacefully surrendering the habit of drinking alcohol. (5 seconds pause)

With each day passing, I notice more constructive changes in my body. (5 seconds pause)

I can effortlessly take control of my habits. (5 seconds pause)

I have a right to be a non-alcoholic person. (5 seconds pause)

I am the chief of my mind and body. (5 seconds pause)

I breathe completely and deeply. (5 seconds pause)

I make the choice to live a healthy lifestyle. (5 seconds pause)

My desire for negative thoughts will pass comfortably. (5 seconds pause)

My blood is full of nutrition and can function properly. (5 seconds pause)

My liver and other organs are healthier than before. (5 seconds pause)

Pause

And now take a minute to acknowledge and appreciate your wonderful life and the phenomenal things that are happening to you.

Alcohol Cessation I

Now that you have total control over your life and you are much motivated, positive and better at taking crucial decisions in your life, things are so better around you!

Your control over your desires and reactions are totally under your control and even the wish for alcohol is controlled by you.

Pause

Alcohol acts as a support for the weak and you are sure that you aren't weak; rather you are upright and confident about yourself and have tremendous will power of the mind. Isn't it?

Pause

There is no one else than yourself that deserves your trust now and you always know that your subconscious mind won't let you down. It will instead guide you towards the right decision in your life and let you do the things which suit the situation to its best.

Pause

The positivity in you is further allowing you to cope with whatever problem that comes in your life. Due to such a drastic change in your attitude, now you have lesser problems in your life too! Your struggling relationships are slowly coming back on track and getting better.

Pause

Yes, you cannot deny it anymore but yes you are moving towards a positive change now and it is helping you to be more relaxed. Your choices are changing and it is making all the difference. The fresh taste of clean water now excites you can makes you feel healthier than before.

The taste of non-alcoholic beverages are being enjoyed by your taste buds and you relish the fact that you are in control- which you lacked some time back. The complete control over your mind and body makes you feel freedom, which is priceless.

Pause

You choose what you eat and drink now. You, with all the senses, choose to only put good and healthy things on your tongue and alcohol is a poison to your health. Be it your brain cells, feelings or your self-respect, alcohol kills it all. Do you really deserve that? No, you deserve greater things in life because you are a great personality and an upbeat human being who is irreplaceable. The feeling of loving yourself more and respecting your dignity is hence very special and dearer to you.

Pause

Do you remember those days when you hardly had any sense about time and date due to the consumption of alcohol? Your voice and body both slurred and you lost every bit of control. The next morning when you woke up, hardly remembering anything of the last night and with a dominating headache due to the hangover- What could you say or do? Did you have a response to these?

Pause

The luring effect of alcohol made you forget everything about your liver, kidneys, stomach and brain and you just couldn't wait to have your next glass of alcohol again.

The good news is that period is over now and you are in total control of yourself. You no longer want to drink alcohol. The simple fact that alcohol is not necessary for healthy living is registered in your mind and hence you are able to live without it.

Pause

Now, imagine yourself with your favourite alcoholic drink- whatever maybe your preference.

Pause

You take the bottle up and the glass body under your fingers feels hard. The bottle is heavier than it felt before and the smell of alcohol is suddenly a lot more unpleasant than it used to be.

Pause

You go straight to the sink and slowly empty the contents of the bottle into the sink with the running water of the tap. The deadly liquid flows out of your bottle and makes it way into the plug-hole and finally disappears. As soon as the alcohol is drained out totally, the desire of your body to have another glass of the fatal drink is surprisingly vanished too!

Pause

Alcohol is the poison your system craves for but your mind denies and hence you say a big NO to it

from now. When you say a NO you stick to it, that's what gentlemen do!
Now you think of a struggling situation in your life when you would have turned to alcohol.

Pause

Feel this for real, note the place of your presence and the companion, sounds and if possible any smell that accompanies this situation.

You know that you can drink alcohol anytime, but it doesn't bother you anymore. It doesn't matter because you are totally free from any addictions or whatsoever. The negative thoughts and the urge to have alcohol is no more present.

Pause

Instead, there's a relaxing sense of confidence and serenity around you just because you have learnt to say NO to alcohol. The feeling of self-respect is worthy and you feel that you are gaining back your lost esteem. Believe that you are a good person to be wit5h and your mind is driven by your powerful will.

Binge Drinking

You currently feel truly good and relaxed - and your inner mind is prepared to acknowledge each suggestion that is presented to you and follow up on it. The suggestions will dive deep into your inward mind and have a prompt and enduring effect on you.

Pause

In addition, since you used to feel awkward drinking liquor, you are here today.

Pause

You have just settled on an awareness level that the time has come to stop drinking - and now we simply need your inner mind to acknowledge your choice.

Get in touch with your awareness and imagine that and the chief and their worker - the manager sits in the workplace throughout the day - orders the workforce to execute them - however a specific representative is not content with a part of their activity - and needs to accomplish something other than what's expected.

They truly attempted to take care of business - however were adjusted to carry out the responsibility a specific way.

Pause

In addition, in light of the fact that the specialists have characterized their job - this rolls out these improvements troublesome - as well as about outlandish - because the chief has not yet concurred.

Indeed - the supervisor doesn't have the foggiest idea about the worker isn't content with what the individual has - on the off chance that the person in question is it is certain they will tune in and give a valiant effort to comprehend.

The supervisor will like the worker and prize him for his drive - through a pay increment or some other advantage.

Pause

It appears as though there was an absence of correspondence between the two - that is the reason now - we will get endorsement from your inner mind - and we are very brave on the most proficient method to push ahead.

Therefore, you've chosen it's an ideal opportunity to connect with the chief - and you need to envision setting off to the workplace and thumping on the entryway.

In the event that it feels great to converse with your chief, you will be brought in.
In addition, when your inner mind is prepared – you will get a signal from your inner mind and you will make a note of it.

Sit tight for a sign.

That is acceptable - presently open the entryway and go in.

You will be approached to plunk down - make your solicitation.

You may quit drinking liquor now?

Pause

On the off chance, that your psyche mind concurs that it will react by imparting a sign to your correct finger - and you can permit that finger to lift. On the off chance, that it does not your inner mind brain will react by imparting a sign to the pointer on the left hand - and you can permit that finger to lift as a sign to me.

Pause

On the off chance that you get no reaction, at that point you should work through whatever obstruction your psyche needs to consent to. Talk about your customer's issue until you get a full understanding.

Pause

Much obliged to you - Now as an arbiter between your brains – it would be preferred to make a proposal on the most proficient method to encourage your new want to quit drinking.

If it is not too much trouble demonstrate yes if both your cognizant and oblivious personalities concur on this.

Pause

What if the psyche is considering helping (customer's name) disregards drinking liquor and exiles any hankering?

Pause

Sit tight for a yes signal - if the appropriate response is no, inquire as to whether it has a superior thought and work with it - expecting proceeded with acknowledgment as follows.

Pause

Much obliged to you subliminal for submitting and consenting to this.

Now, as is it tallied down from ten to one - you will twofold your unwinding score with each number that is being checked.

Ten - twofold this unwinding - nine - twofold unwinding again - eight - more profound, more profound and more profound - seven - six - continue multiplying this unwinding - five - twofold solace - four - loosen up twice - three - more profound still - two - and one.

You will see that starting now and into the foreseeable future you can disregard drinking alcohol - just overlook drinking it.

Have you at any point had the experience of going into a space for something and when you arrive - overlook what you went for?

This is actually, what it resembles now with drinking liquor - essentially neglect to drink it.

In addition, it's so natural to overlook - similarly as you neglected to put your shoes on now - to remind you.

Pause

On the off chance that the possibility of alcohol gets into your psyche - you will overlook it in a split second - and it is simple like A B C - to overlook - and accomplish something other than what's expected - have a ton of fun.

Furthermore, when you neglect to drink liquor - you find that you are compensated from multiple points of view - better wellbeing - more pride - additional cash - a lovely sentiment of certainty - sharpness and concentrate constantly - on the grounds that you are liberated from drinking limitations. A great deal!

Pause

Consistently you feel much improved, more advantageous, more joyful and more in charge.

You feel good - but then - in entrancing - you feel superbly loose and loose.

Social Drinking

You are currently profoundly feeling relaxed and are agreeable, and your mind is open and responsive to the suggestions you are going to hear.

Pause

You are tuning in to me today since you understand that you have been drinking more alcohol off late than you needed to - and now you need to make another, more advantageous example of essentially having an odd mixed beverage when you're in social situations.

So first, it is important to compliment you for settling on this choice - because it shows that you truly comprehend the risks of getting dependent on liquor.

Pause

It is certain that you understand – extreme consumption of alcohol is a toxic to your body - it can cause issues with your liver, kidneys, stomach, and heart.

Pause

Liquor can likewise influence your ordinary everyday life - particularly when individuals lose their inhibitions.

Pause

It can likewise influence social, work, and general personal satisfaction - and obviously - the principal thing alcohol hinders your reasoning and feeling of judgment - no big surprise it has frequently alluded to as Satan's beverage.

However, you are putting the entirety of this behind you, and starting now and into the foreseeable future you will restrict your liquor use so you generally fall inside the suggested rules.

Pause

You will likewise quit drinking alcohol at home - aside from where conceivable in specific circumstances - maybe in the event that you are inviting visitors or praising an exceptionally unique occasion.

In any case - you may find that you hate it a similar way you used to - and that is all right - on the grounds that you are more joyful when you are in finished control and your reasoning is sound.

The main thing you choose to do is to quit purchasing the containers, jars of wine, spirits, or lager - or some other mixed drink - and you will be wonderfully be shocked at the fact that it is so natural to do as such.

Envision the store or store where you go to purchase the liquor.

Pause

Perhaps you can see the store name on the whiteboard - simply take a cloth or eraser and wipe it off - the truth is out - simply wipe that store from your mind. When the board turns out to be clear so you can inhale a murmur of alleviation - as though that specific store does not exist anymore - and it does not exist anymore - at the forefront of your thoughts.

Pause

Since it is so natural to overlook the things we need to overlook - rather we recall why we decided to overlook them.

In the event that you ordinarily purchase alcohol nearby other markets - for instance a general store - at that point you need to envision this grocery store now. Recall his name and see the grocery store in your inner being.

Pause

At this point, you presumably know this store quite well - and in all probability you know its plan - where products of the soil are kept - where there are bread and cakes - the solidified nourishments segment and the various things that your general store sells.

Pause

At a certain point, you knew precisely where the wine, brew, spirits and other liquor path was found - however now you couldn't care less - so perhaps you can envision it simply isn't there any longer.

Pause

Furthermore, when you visit that store to do the shopping - you walk straight through the passageway - not in any event, seeing - you certainly couldn't care less - where it is - or not.

Pause

Furthermore, - on the off chance that you are having some good times or if there is an extraordinary occasion whereby you feel that you should serve liquor to your visitors - maybe you can approach another person to get it for you - on the grounds that you would truly lean toward not to go down this way.

Since you have quit purchasing liquor to drink at home, it will be a lot simpler for you to shed it.

In addition, obviously - you may have essentially become acclimated to drinking - for this situation how about we make a more significant elective propensity.

Also, there is a lot to look over - there is such a great amount to do.

You can gain proficiency with another aptitude, read your preferred books, paint, draw, or sew.

You can begin another leisure activity, fabricate models, become familiar with a language, and compose your biography or any number of fascinating things.

.

Pause

In the event that you for the most part drink alcohol late around evening time, you may now need to appreciate early evenings in bed - get a decent rest and rest or invest energy with your cherished one.

Pause

In addition, it's astounding how you locate that after only a couple of long periods of not drinking - the possibility of that appears to have vanished from your brain - you don't need it now - you needn't bother with it.

Indeed, even in social circumstances, you may find that you are not as distracted from the reality as you used to be with liquor.

Pause

You frequently lean toward a soda pop that you know is better for you and will last more.

Starting now and into the foreseeable future, liquor has lost its significance to you. You cannot envision what it probably been similar to when you drank at home - all you truly know is that you will be so glad to stop.

Pause

These proposals are immovably inserted in your mind and develop more grounded and more grounded step by step.

Get more grounded constantly, more grounded continuously, and more grounded constantly.

Alcohol Cessation ii

Individuals with liquor issues frequently need assistance with their confidence and some type of certainty building. Set aside some effort to discover what you are good at, and carry your benevolent sentiments into play with a physical reaction, for example, tightening your right hand fist. This will help direct consideration away from the inside reaction and engage you with the positive feelings.

Pause

"For quite a while now you have been acting and feeling in manners that separated you from your ordinary self. You have been increasingly dependent more on alcohol to assist you with defeating the negative emotions you have been encountering, and you have done as such to the point that you wind up denying yourself your actual feelings. Isn't it?

Pause

No one feels large and in charge constantly and there will be days that could be better for you. Just by encountering a portion of the lows in life, can you really appreciate and welcome the highs.

Eradicating your feelings with alcohol doesn't explain anything, it just exacerbates the situation, which is the reason you've chosen to listen to this audio. You have had enough liquor, and you truly need to help take care of your old issues.

Concentrate now on an aspect of your life that you feel cheerful in - you might need to recall something great that happened, something that caused you to feel certain, maybe an accomplishment or some amazing feeling of accomplishment or pride (Pause) ... presently notice how you feel inside, pride, certainty, and bliss - and let those nice feelings and thoughts to become more grounded, while you relax and let go.

Pause

Furthermore, when these positive emotions and feelings fill you, you need to take a full breath and tighten your right hand fist, while your inner mind safeguards those nice feelings and locks them in.

That's right.

Since when you like to feel as such, you should simply take a long full breath and tighten your right hand fist. Every time in future when you are stressed or feeling overwhelmed with the negative emotions, simply tighten your right hand fist.

Pause

Notice the feelings within you when think of having a drink and go to the bar or kitchen to grab a glass, you need to take a full breath through your nose and tighten your right hand fist while you recollect those positive, sure emotions.

Pause

You promptly feel better. It is a great idea to be certain and realize that you are liberated from the old, addictive lifestyle. Liberated from the weight of drinking alcohol, allowed to proceed with your awesome life, to encounter the highs, just as the lows, realizing this will push you to genuinely acknowledge when things improve.

Pause

You are evolving. Your perspective improves, your authority, you assume responsibility, you are in charge. You are completely liberated, liberated from the addictive way of life, and truly, there will be minutes where you feel torment, yet these minutes will diminish to an ever increasing extent, and you will truly value the pleasant things in life the easily overlooked details that cause you grin and to feel cheerful.

Alcohol Session III

Presently as you move further and into the profound relaxation ... more deeper, more relaxed...you notice all sounds blurring away and you just focus on the sound of my voice. Going further down and down, deeper and deeper. There are three stages to disposing of any alcohol issue. The initial step is relaxation and you are relaxing already.

Pause

Clearly, you must be relaxed and you are not totally relaxing in every way and in every shape or form right now, currently you need to totally unwind ... relinquish everything.

Let your arms and legs and your whole body completely go relax. Since you are relaxed than you were previously, the second point to quit alcohol is understanding the "why" of having alcohol. In addition, you completely comprehend it as a matter of first importance, in every occurrence of a drinking issue in your mind. The individual who tends to drink too much, including yourself, has been defined in your mind.

Pause

It could be someone in your family or your close friend who you relate to when you drink. Or maybe the reason is something else. If it is someone you know who has been a heavy drinker, then today is the day to simply cut the cords with that person. You do not need to be like him or her. You just need to be the real you. The one who wants to quit alcohol and is listening to this recording. This person is going to cut the cords with that person who perhaps introduced you to it or who you relate to more.

Pause

In a moment, in your imagination, I would like you to call that person and imagine a white cord being connected between the two of you. You notice the elastic white thick cord connecting you both and you notice it between the torsos.

Today is the day to let go of that person from your mind and spirit by cutting the cord. I would like you to imagine cutting the cord with a big garden shear. As you cut it, you notice the person leaves you and goes far and far away from you.

Pause (10 seconds)

That's right.

You are free from it. You are free from the energetic connection with that person from your life…who is a heavy drinker and you somehow relate to them.

Pause

The third stage is to remember the god or the higher power or the one you believe in. Just remember that and surrender. Surrender all your worries to him and you shall feel lighter and much more relaxed.

Everything will be taken care by the supreme power or whoever you believe in. Just trust the process of life and trust the one you believe in and you will be able to kick off this old habit.

Alcohol Session IV

You continue to drift into a deep relaxed state of mind, and as you drift deeper, you can hear my voice a lot clearer. You can see all other distractions slowly fading away. We are now going to help you get rid of all the suggestions in your mind.

Pause

And as you listen carefully, we will rid your mind from each and every negative suggestion now and forever. You are now completely focused on my voice and nothing can distract you in any way. You completely accept everything I say to you because everything I say is the absolute truth. We are going to rid your mind of every suggestion that has been detrimental to your well-being.

Pause

The first suggestion we are going to rid your mind of is alcohol. In the past you enjoyed drinking because you thought it made you feel better but now you know that the reality is far from it. You now know that alcohol is of no use to you . You do not need alcohol for any reason anymore. It doesn't help you relax and on the contrary it affects your sleep. Alcohol does you absolutely no good.

Pause

As a matter of fact, alcohol ruins your efficiency and since you have realised, you have now overcome the need for alcohol. And through this we have completely eradicated any suggestion of alcohol being beneficial to you. I am going to count to five and from that moment on, the suggestion that alcohol is beneficial to you will no longer exist in your mind.

One, two, three, four, five.

Pause

Let's move on to the next suggestion which is using alcohol to punish yourself. You no longer need alcohol to punish yourself because you have realised you don't need to punish yourself anymore. People only punish themselves because somewhere deep in their minds they feel guilty and you have now overcome this - you no longer allow yourself to feel guilty.

Pause

We are now going to empty your mind of all forms of guilt and along with that we will eliminate the need for you to punish yourself by consuming alcohol.

One, two, three, four, five.

And that suggestion has now been emptied from your mind. You now understand that alcohol is poisonous. It makes you sick and inefficient and so you have overcome the need to poison yourself.

One, two, three, four, five.

It's now time to rid your mind of all connections to alcohol. The only kind of alcohol you know or care about is rubbing alcohol. Rubbing Alcohol is wonderful, it's great to use for a nice back rub and that's the only use it has in your life.

Pause

You no longer associate alcohol as a beverage. The only alcohol you are aware of is Rubbing Alcohol and therefore we have rid your mind of all connections to alcohol as a beverage. You no longer think of alcohol as a beverage. You don't ask for it, you don't need it or desire it in any form. Even if you were offered alcohol, you would refuse it because you find alcohol disgusting. It tastes terrible and it makes you puke. Now, at the count of five, we are going to eradicate all negative suggestions from your mind and replace them with the new positive suggestion I have given you.

One, two, three, four, five.

From this moment on you are completely free from alcohol and it's entangling octopus like tentacles. You are free from it's self-punishing nature, free from it's clutches which was ruining your life. You are completely free because all the connections in your mind to alcohol have been emptied. We have unplugged the wires and it's not possible to ever restore it even if you would want to.

Imagine there's a huge telephone switchboard inside your head and all the wires connected to the socket marked "alcohol" are now removed and it won't work even if you try plugging it back in.

Pause

Alcohol disgusts you. You no longer want to buy it and even if someone offers you alcohol you decline because it has a foul taste. It has a terrible effect on you and makes you very uncomfortable to even think about it.

One, two, three, four, five.

Now you are completely free of the alcohol problem in every way. You are surprised and amazed by your self-discipline and confidence knowing that you have overcome your alcohol problem forever. Now sleep, sleep deeply and let your mind concentrate on the sound of my voice as you go deeper and deeper into a relaxed state of mind.

Alcohol Session V

Now, let me tell you how alcohol is poison for individuals with a drinking problem. It's poisonous in two ways.

Pause

Firstly, it's a psychological poison as it weakens your willpower, your ego and the faith in yourself. To give you an example, if you ever go back to drinking after overcoming the alcohol problem; you will notice negative thoughts & feelings returning to your mind. Thoughts such as "I'm good for nothing", "I really don't like myself'" and so on.

Pause

Secondly, it's physical poison because you are now allergic to alcohol similar to how people have other allergies. And once you're allergic to something, even if it's something like penicillin, it's going to be poisonous to your system and you must never consume it. The same now applies to alcohol.

Pause

And so, since you are allergic to alcohol you no longer need it. Alcohol is poison to you.

Here's another interesting fact - people who are drawn to alcohol never really say good things about alcohol. You don't hear them say things like "It makes me feel good" or "I like the taste of it".

Pause

In fact, they speak of it in exactly the opposite manner. They say things like " I don't like it, it's terrible", "It's ruining my life". So why are they drawn to it even after knowing alcohol is not good for them? It's because in their subconscious mind they want to commit suicide, and so they use alcohol to punish themselves in a slow tortorous way.

Now that you understand this, you can see why it is so important to eradicate the underlying problem - that is the issue of punishing oneself.

Pause

We have therefore rid your mind of all the guilt, and since you are no longer guilty, there is no need to punish yourself anymore.

Let us leave that in the hands of the higher power.

From this moment on, you no longer need to punish or poison yourself. You realise alcohol is poison and you are therefore going to leave that poison alone. You don't need to punish or poison yourself anymore because you have rid yourself of such negative thoughts & suggestions.

You are now going to start appreciating yourself, you are going to appreciate the talents you have. You are going to acknowledge that you are special in your own way and you will appreciate the good life you have been given. You will now begin to see all the good deeds you can do in your life for yourself and for others.

Pause

There are certain terms that are synonymous with alcohol. Terms lie "He certainly got stiff"' which is also used to describe a dead man. We also hear people use the term "Dead Drunk". It's interesting how the terms dead & drunk are often used together, isn't it?

Pause

It's because alcohol is poison, and you are now able to understand and see how alcohol is poison and therefore you are completely free and you no longer have the need for alcohol. In fact, you can't even smell it anymore.

Pause

You are just beginning to appreciate and value yourself. You are beginning to take good care of your mind and body. You are going to stay sober and by doing that you will make yourself and everyone else happy.

You will avoid alcohol like the plague. You will avoid it cause it's a substance that you are most allergic to.

Pause

And by avoiding alcohol, you have won a significant battle in your life and it's now forever placed behind you. You now have a beautiful future ahead of you and no matter what obstacle may come your way in the future, it will still be easier for you to face those challenges sober. You are going to be happier and have twice as much fun sober than you ever had when you used to be drunk.

Pause

Alcohol was only poisoning your system. It was killing you slowly but surely and it almost succeeded but you managed to rid your mind of all those thoughts and today you no longer see the need to punish yourself.

Pause

You are now going to start appreciating yourself and you are going to become stronger and be happier.

You no longer need to punish yourself. Now take a deep breath and with every breath you will feel yourself going into a deeper relaxed state of mind and all these new positive suggestions will be reinforced in your mind every single day of your life.

Way to Sobriety

You continue to drift deeper and deeper into a much more peaceful state and as you continue to do so, I wonder if you can imagine a big library somewhere. It could be a library that you want to create now in your mind or the library you have been before.

Pause (10 seconds)

That's right.

The library that you notice has many many books on many many shelves. And as you continue to look at the books on many shelves, you notice a shelf that has the books of your life.

Pause

That shelf has books from your life and each book has every little moment of your life that you have already lived. I wonder if you can take a closer look at the shelf with the books from your life now.

Pause

And as you take a closer look at the long shelf of books from your life, you notice that the right side of the shelf has all the inspiring and happy books. The books that have the positive moments of your life. You touch them and feel the texture of each of the book. You notice the colour and the cover page. Are they paper back or hard covered?

Notice..

Just get the knowing of each of the book as you continue to take a closer look at the right side of the shelf. Each of the books on the right side contains your goals, accomplishments, dreams, and good memories. These books have all the amazing things you have done in life and all the good things you plan to do in your life. All the positive emotions you have ever experienced with all the positive people. The right is the positive side.

Pause

The books on the right side also contains information about your talents and skills. This is the side of books that you are truly proud of you. You have achieved so much, you are amazing and good enough. It has the books from the times when you were appreciated, whether it was your school or home or work. Every book on the right side of the shelf has a positive story from your life. It also has books that describe your true nature and your personality. You are amazed at the collection of books and the information available inside.

Pause

The other side of the shelf, which is the left side has books that perhaps contain not so good memories from your life. Here, you will notice books that contain incidents and stories of the times, where you felt low, sad, angry, in the events you feel should not have really happened to you.

Pause

When you further look at the books on the left, you notice the shelf also has books about the various problems you faced in your life – whether emotional, financial, physical. All the books here are just opposite to the books on the right side of the shelf.

Pause

These are the books that sometimes hold you back in the past and do not do any good to you. These are the memories that serve no purpose and you sometimes seem to stay stuck in them, thinking about whys and hows of every situation.

Pause

Come to think of it, you have probably been reading just the negative books on the left and especially when you are drinking.

What do you get out of reading them? Sadness and negativity, isn't it?

Pause

It's been so many years that you have just been reading these negative books and you know there's no positive learning coming from them. They make you sad or perhaps angry. Whatever emotion you get when you read them, you know is is negative. Isn't it?

You have carried them along for too long. The time has come to discard them coz they do not add any value to you and your life.

You have decided to let go of all these books and decided to discard them in the trash can. Just outside the main door of the library, there is an extra-large trash can ready to take in all the old worn out negative books from the left side of the shelf.

Pause

You now go back to the shelf and take a carry basket to put in all the negative books holding every negative emotion and memory from your past that serve no purpose and make you feel sad.

Put them one by one in the carry basket.

Pause (10 seconds)

Now, take all those books to the big trash can and start dumping the books one by one into it.

Pause (10 seconds)

That's right.

And as you see the books in the trash can, you start to feel positivity encompassing you from all side. It feels as if the weight has been lifted up from your shoulders.

You go back to the shelf just to see if there are any more books that need to be discarded.

Pause

You take a closer look again and you notice that you have missed a few books that also contains your worries and stresses about future. And you know that you cannot let go of your present day thinking or worrying about the future.

And, there is no point in worrying, instead, you can plan and you can plan for the plan a and plan b so that you know that if something goes wrong, you know exactly what you need to do.

So, pick up those books and put them in the carry basket and dump them in the trash can, just outside the library.

Pause (10 seconds)

That's right.

Great job done! This is another step to loving yourself and knowing that you are full of love and give yourself all the care and attention. You have just gotten rid yourself of all the baggage that served no purpose.

You feel even more lighter now and as you were picking up the last set of books to discard, you noticed that there was a large hard covered book also lying on the shelf.

And, that got you curious and you perhaps thought that it's the book on the right, but it is lying just in the centre that divides the shelf in left and right.

You go back and pick that heavy book and open it to read the table of contents.

And, you notice that this books is about the problem behaviour, the book of alcoholism and this book contains everything you have done under the influence of alcohol, it may contain good memories but majorly it has bad memories.

You have decided to get rid of the book too so that you can only have a shelf of positive books in the library.

Take it in your hands and move towards the trash can. (Pause)

Move towards it with the book in your hand and simply throw it in the trash can.

You don't need it…at all.

Pause

You now go back to the shelf to check out the right side of the shelf. And, in those books, one book catch your attention that says : "My Book of Sobriety"

You take that book out and feel the texture of the book and smell it.

Pause

You decide to take a look at it and for that you look for a comfy chair to sit in the library. In a moment, you notice a comfy couch for you to sit and read the book.

You take a seat and rest in the chair and as you flip the pages, your conscious mind begin to drift away in the distance while the subconscious mind pays starts to pay attention to every word written in the book.

And as you begin to read, your subconscious mind opens itself to absorb the wisdom and knowledge. Whatever idea is written in the book, your subconscious mind happily and willingly accepts them.

Pause

You know that you are powerful to overcome any addiction or habit. You are much more powerful than your own thoughts and you can control them easily. You look forward to living a fulfilling and healthy life and you can achieve that by being sober. To have a thriving life, you embrace health and healthy foods and drinks. And, as you continue to eat and drink healthy, you begin to notice positive change in your sleeping and eating pattern. You begin to notice change in your environment.

I would like you to now embrace this beautiful and positive change and let your inner mind fill itself with the wisdom from the book.

I would be quite for a few moments.

Pause (25 seconds)

Now, come back to each word I say now. You are beginning to live a new life, a healthier and more successful life. You are a child of god and you believe in the process of life. You trust yourself, the god, and the process of life.

Pause

Now, simply continue to breathe and each breath you take strengthens each wisdom and word from the book. And the book says this beautiful prayer that you will embrace for the rest of your life and it goes like this:
Give me the serenity to accept the things I cannot change, the strength and courage to change the things I can, and the wisdom to know the difference.

With this, you look at the shelf of positive books from your life and feel positive and completely motivated to live a healthier and even better life from now on.

Healing the Past

You are relaxing your mind and taking deep breaths, with each soft, pleasant rhythmic breath, you are becoming calmer and relaxing more deeply. While breathing out, you are exhaling out all your stress, negativity, tension, discomfort. And during inhaling of each breath, you are inviting all the positive energy, calmness and peace into your mind and body.

Pause

You relax more deeply with each cycle of breath, your inner mind is much stronger and approachable to all the specific, beneficial ideas in this recording. With every single breath and beat of your heart, the mind is absorbing each positive suggestion for the purpose of healing. Your mind is absorbing these suggestions and building them as your inner and outer reality.

Pause

Your heart is having a beautiful place like a meadow, just like the place in the outer world. And the feelings are the same in the outer world or inner world. When you visit the inner meadow of heart, you are getting in a place of safety and flexibility. There you can be cheerful. It is always there for you. For visiting the meadow you don't have to listen to this recording really. It's a place where you don't require such things. All you have to do is just close your eyes, feel safe and you will be in the meadow.

Pause

As you are thinking about the meadow, a wave of stillness, calmness fills your mind. This feeling is not for a particular moment, beside it is deep and long-lasting regardless of what is happening around you.

Pause

You are now allowing your outer conscious mind to relax in the meadow and drift in the calmness and serenity. While the inner mind is doing all this work. The outer mind is listening to the instructions and following, the inner mind is the one that is doing the work.

That's right.

Pause

You may have experienced a lot of emotional pain and trauma in the past. The memories of that past are still with you and are present with you in your life. It is not only affecting physically but also mentally. All it is doing is just filling your current life with pain and fear, and inhibiting your choices in life.

While listening to this recording you are guiding your inner mind that the time has arrived to heal the pain you have been suffering. And its time you should live your life perfect and positively as you deserve.

When we experience a negative event, it causes emotional injury and if it causes tremendous pain than what we can handle at that time, it actually ruptures our mind.

Our mind is a great device if such issue is present it will keep that sensitive part in one corner of the mind and locks it so that we can grow and survive through it.

No doubt it is a constructive strategy that we can continue to live our lives with such immense pain that is so big to bear. Despite this, the pain is still inside us. That budding, sensitive part of the mind is still experiencing the same emotional pain, shame, anxiety, fright most of the times.

Pause

So the first step to healing for the mind and soul is to protect that younger budding part of the mind. You don't have to recall or look back to all those memories of past in detail even though you may remember some peculiar parts of it. But you don't have to worry as you are ready to cope up with it easily.

Pause

These memories are in your subconscious mind and that is why the healing will take place in your subconscious, underneath the surface. For the healing, all you have to know is that there is this small younger part of the mind that is still entrapped in old bad memories which are excruciating the pain in your present life.

Pause

Now imagine yourself as that child, it is not necessary that you have some remembrance of that time. You have to imagine your younger self in some kind of negative emotion.

Get the knowing of that negative emotion. It could be any emotion.

together with all your grownup strength get that child up and cradle the younger self with warmth and affection in your arms. And tell that child that " You are safe and protected now, no one can harm you... I am your future self. I am here to help you."

With the courage and stability deep-rooted in you have taken the younger self out from the old bad memories. You let him know that "You don't have to live that painful life ever again in future".

Pause

As you are strong enough it will be your decision to go back to those memories, but you don't have to live it again. And please notice the sign of happiness, satisfaction at the face of your younger self. Just by looking at the innocent face, you feel relaxed.

Now allow your younger self to move to the beautiful meadow of mind, the place of bliss and joy. Younger self will never face any pain in life again because you are always there ..the capable, wise adult. you are not only there to get through the challenges of life but you are there to blossom with every experience.

You convey the child the message that it has to explore the interest, pride, playfulness, cheerfulness of youth and return this contribution to the outer world.

Pause

At this moment you and your younger self are standing in the meadow, and you notice that sunset is going to happen. As you see the beautiful nightfall, you start to understand that this is the time when you will let all the injuries, the pain of the prior life into the past and make your upcoming life unbound to these bad memories.

Pause

With the sunset in your meadow, you are choosing a new path of life and letting these old issues disappear.

Imagine the Sun going down….and as it goes down, you let all the old emotional baggage disappear.

That's right.

You are completely enjoying the marvellous moment of sunset with all the ethnic group of colours orange, blue, red that are painting the sky. You notice the appealing light dancing in the clouds like waves and spraying all colours on you and your meadow. You are enthralled by the light and you feel this energy inside your life. By this energy, you can feel a sudden powerful upward movement and healing of the inner soul.

Pause

You grant the old memories to vanish from your life and become insignificant. these memories are just some old incident in the road of your life and they are fading into the past. And there is an old fashioned saying that "whatever doesn't kill us makes us stronger". By this time you can easily understand that you are a survivor and this has made you much strong, tough, buoyant, concerned human being. Till sunset, you are feeling more strengthened and refreshed.

You can witness your younger self relaxing, inclining towards the healing and regenerating sleep after so many years. The old soreness is dissolving away with sunset.

Pause

Straightaway I will ask you to do something challenging but the radiance of the moon in the meadow will make this challenge easy.

You have to forgive the individual or people who injured you emotionally.

Remember that forgiving someone doesn't mean that the incident never happened. It means that you will make a clear borderline so that it will not happen to you again. And if the person continues to harm you then you will take all emotional, communal, legal actions to stop them.

Pause

The main motive of forgiveness is that you will not have any bitterness, rage, uneasiness, vengeance in your heart for that person. It will not poison your heart.

Imagine the person who has hurt you is sitting on a chair, and he or she is listening to you. Then you will let them realize the pain, and details of how they hurt you and the consequences you are facing because of them. The damage they made was affecting your present.

Pause

Tell them your boundaries and that such wrong behaviour is never approved again. Let them listen to all your injury, pain and suffer. They should understand the pain they gave you not as vengeance, but directly so they realize what they did to you. PAUSE for 10 seconds.

Pause

Just give them a chance to reply. PAUSE 10 seconds..... Regardless whatever they reply or if they apologize, convey them again what is acceptable or not acceptable to you, and also that they can never harm you again....PAUSE 10 seconds..

That's right

Now you have defined your boundaries so let us return back to our peaceful meadow, free of the people who hurt you. You let go all your vengeance, anger, pain, fear in past. You will now loosen those people who hurt you and free up them. You can freely now explore new, healthy and trustworthy relationships in life. And the people who didn't apologize you will let them disappear.

Pause

The delicate moonlight is filling your meadow with magical healing light. Your younger self is sleeping freely to wake up on the new day of healing.

You are enjoying the moment of radiance. This radiance is comforting, soft and healing even more than you can imagine. All you can feel is light-hearted, free of all the anguish. Fear, anger, shame these are long gone from your life. Your heart and mind are stress-free and light, they are so light as if you can imagine yourself flying.

Pause

After all this, you realize that your life is completely changed and you are grateful. Now you can achieve all the happiness you deserve without any obstacles.

You recognize that the new sunrise will be a new beginning for your life that will make accessible all the positivity to you. The injured part is healing with every breath you are taking.

Pause

If the suggestions and ideas of this recording are adequate to you then you keep on breathing. The more you will listen to this recording the faster and quickly you will relax and heal.

As you keep visiting your meadow either by listening to this recording or just by closing your eyes the more confidence, serene, harmony will flow to your outer mind. You are a completely new human being who is happier, contented, subtle, and powerful , living in this wonderful world.

Pause

You are adored and cherished with every passing day as you heal more deeply your internal and external worlds become delightful.

Exploring Coping Strategies

And you can overcome this addiction of consuming excessive alcohol in your own way and in your own time and a part of you know knows exactly why you have it when you do not want to have it.

Your mind can explore whether it's a pattern of behaviour that has its roots in the past or whether it's just a coping mechanism to some other problem. And just how when you get a set of new clothes and change your wardrobe, you stop using the old clothes and perhaps discard them.

And, similarly, when you accept a new way of living, you discard the old way of living and this new life could be full of health, motivations, rewards, goals, accomplishments, success, love, and laughter,

Pause

All the positive change that you desire will be in line with the person you are, having a positive influence on yourself and the people around you. And, you will be a new person, a healthy and happy person as if you are wearing a new suit with an absolutely new makeover.

The time has come to take back control from the old part of you that was sticking with the old habit serving no purpose really.

Pause

Perhaps it served some purpose in the past and I would like to say thanks to that part of you which perhaps served some kind of purpose for your good, when perhaps you could not think of better ways to cope up with things you needed to cope up with. But, with me, you can explore many possibilities and new ways to live a healthier life and cope up with difficulties through better ways.

Pause

Some of the coping strategies that will help you in difficult situations are breathing exercises. Breathing always helps as it ground you and aligns your emotional and mental bodies. Every time you are stressed, simply take deep breaths and with every breath you take, you will feel much relaxed and calmer.

Take 7 to 10 deep breaths and you will be much more calmer.

Another coping strategy is to be mindful and involve all your five senses to bring your thoughts back to the present moment, without judging yourself.

Here, are some ways to do so…

Remember the 54321 technique, where at 5, you look at the five different things around you, 4 touch the four different things around you, 3, you listen to three different sounds or noises around you, at 2, you smell two different smells…it could be your natural body odour, a book lying near you, or anything you notice that may have a smell. 1, you taste one thing. When this happens, you involve all your five senses and bring your thoughts back to the present moment. This is especially useful when you are constantly worrying about future or nervous about something…and overwhelmed by the thoughts about future…

Pause

The next coping strategy is to say the serenity prayer and surrender everything to god and continue to trust the process of life.

Repeat after me three times :

Give me the serenity to accept the things I cannot change (**Pause)** the strength and courage to change the things I can (**Pause)**
and the wisdom to know the difference (**Pause**)

Pause

Give me the serenity to accept the things I cannot change (**Pause)** the strength and courage to change the things I can (**Pause)**
and the wisdom to know the difference (**Pause**)

Give me the serenity to accept the things I cannot change (**Pause)** the strength and courage to change the things I can (**Pause)**
and the wisdom to know the difference (**Pause**)

That's right.

Sleep Better

As you continue to relax and continue to listen to each word I say, you further drift deeper into a beautiful state of relaxation. And with this, you feel the sense of confidence that you will fall asleep easily and every time you decide to sleep.

Pause

As you are relaxed now, it is easier for you to fall asleep and every day when you relax yourself like this, you would easily and instantly fall into the deepest and restful slumber.

Deep relaxation is the prelude to the beautiful sleep and you inform your subconscious mind how much you desire to sleep better so that you wake up feeling fresh, alert, and happy.

And, as you continue to listen to each word I say, every word makes a powerful impact on your subconscious and allows it to do whatever healthy and powerful things it takes you to achieve your goal of sleeping fast and peacefully as soon as you lay on the bed with the goal to sleep and achieve a restful sleep.

Pause

And with each breath and every rise and fall of your chest, all these words and your thoughts about achieving a restful sleep get magnified and locked in your powerful subconscious mind.

You inform your subconscious mind the goal and why is it important for you to sleep on time.

Pause

The goal is to sleep fully and deeply without night time awakenings unless the nature calls so that you wake up feeling totally refreshed and energetic.

Your creative and powerful mind is listening to me and locking in these ideas to implement them when you are up and awake.

Pause

And, I am going to be taking to that part of you now about the first idea that will help you fall asleep easily. And, that sleep is natural and effortless. It is not to be tried, it is to be allowed. Every human and animal sleeps because it is natural. However, some of us may have difficulty falling asleep because we get confused between naturally sleeping and trying to sleep, and because trying requires an effort, and making an effort causes us to stay up.

Today is the day to understand this idea and implement it. From now on, you do not try but allow yourself to get completely relaxed and flow gently into the state of mind just how you are relaxed now to promote sleep.

And, I wonder if you could now imagine a beautiful garden, the garden you feel is safe and been to before. Or maybe, you want to imagine an absolutely new garden that is safe, secure, and beautiful to look at.

Pause (10 seconds)

And, as you imagine this beautiful garden, I would like you to look around and see the beautiful trees, the lush green grass, the colours of the sky and feel the pleasant breeze. Perhaps you can even smell the moss and the fresh air.

It looks beautiful around and you feel absolutely wonderful, isn't it?

Maybe some time ago, there was a part of you which became fearful of sleeping for whatever reasons or maybe you did not want to lose control and wanted to control sleep. The reasons could be many. And, perhaps that was the best solution you found to cope with something….the solution of not falling asleep. But this was long time ago and now you know the importance of sleeping every night.

Therefore, you allow yourself to let the past fade away….as if you are leaving everything behind you and entering a tunnel to a brighter and new side.

Pause

The new side is the new day where you begin to feel and think different about sleep. The new life where you sleep peacefully every night and wake up feeling fresh and energised the next morning.

I want you to imagine that now…

And, as you imagine this new day with a new beginning, you find yourself swinging in a hammock tied between two trees.

You allow yourself to completely relax as you enjoy each swing from right to left and left to right…

And you look at the Sun going down….and the birds chirping….and it starts to get dark around you….

Pause (10 seconds)

So, let's move into sleep, and as I say that, I mean you focus on breath and the rise and fall of your chest. And as you focus on the breath, you count yourself down from 20 down to 0, continuing to feel smooth and rhythmic breath you feel moving in through your nose and moving out of your mouth.

That's right…

And with each count down, you will drift into a deeper state of relaxation

20…..19……18…….17……...16…….15………14…………...13………12………11……drifting deeper and deeper….10…..9……8……7…..6……5…….4……3…….2……1…0…..

Pause

And this how you fall into a deep slumber every night….and every time you lay on the bed for the purpose of sleeping, you imagine this beautiful garden, the lush green garden with beautiful sky and find yourself in a hammock.

And as you swing in it, you begin to notice the rise and fall of your chest as you breathe and with every swing from left to right and right to left, you count down from 20 down to 0….and you will notice the sun going down and it goes down, you notice yourself drifting into a beautiful state of mind, which is deep and restful sleep.

Affirmations

1. You are getting healthier (7 seconds pause)
2. You breathe better and your health is getting better (7 seconds pause)
3. You love your body and you take utmost care of it (7 seconds pause)
4. You look forward to living an alcohol-free life (7 seconds pause)
5. You dislike the taste of alcohol (7 seconds pause)
6. Alcohol remind you of liver failure and all the costs that come with it (7 seconds pause)
7. You enjoy being sober (7 seconds pause)
8. You love yourself unconditionally (7 seconds pause)
9. You save money as a sober person (7 seconds pause)
10. You love yourself (7 seconds pause)
11. You love your body (7 seconds pause)
12. You want to live a long life (7 seconds pause)
13. You want to enjoy the gifts of life (7 seconds pause)
14. You drink 8 to 10 glasses of water everyday (7 seconds pause)

15. You take care of your health everyday (7 seconds pause)
16. You love to exercise (7 seconds pause)
17. You sleep on time and take care of your sleep cycle (7 seconds pause)
18. Your feel energetic as a sober (7 seconds pause)
19. Your skin glows with health and radiance (7 seconds pause)
20. You breathe fresh air (7 seconds pause)
21. You have more interesting things to do in life now (7 seconds pause)
22. You love all the time you have to be productive and to learn new things in life (7 seconds pause) (7 seconds pause)
23. You feel amazing as an individual (7 seconds pause)
24. Your self love and self-appreciation has increased (7 seconds pause)
25. You respect your body, mind, and soul (7 seconds pause)
26. Everyday, you are feeling healthier and happier (7 seconds pause)
27. You prefer to have soft drinks when you go out and socialise (7 seconds pause)
28. You choose to live as sober. (7 seconds pause)
29. You choose to not drink and feel great about yourself (7 seconds pause)

30. You live a beautiful life (7 seconds pause)
31. Your liver and other organs are feeling great with every passing day (7 seconds pause)
32. You love your family (7 seconds pause)
33. You have a deep love for your body (7 seconds pause)
34. Your self-esteem improves with every passing day (7 seconds pause)
35. Your health is improving with every passing day (7 seconds pause)
36. You are able to taste food better (7 seconds pause)
37. You are much calmer and relaxed (7 seconds pause)
38. Your relationships improve with every passing day completely (7 seconds pause)
39. You see a positive change in people around you (7 seconds pause)
40. You sleep better and fall asleep faster (7 seconds pause)
41. You have taken charge of your health and body and that makes you feel amazing (7 seconds pause)
42. You are happy and positive (7 seconds pause)
43. You are proud of yourself to have overcome alcohol addiction (7 seconds pause)

44. You are stronger than a hard drink (7 seconds pause)
45. You are the master of your mind (7 seconds pause)
46. You have control on your thoughts (7 seconds pause)
47. You are proud to have a healthy lifestyle (7 seconds pause)
48. You inspire people (7 seconds pause)
49. You breathe better (7 seconds pause)
50. You breathe fresh air (7 seconds pause)
51. You are stronger than any habit (7 seconds pause)
52. You can change habits easily (7 seconds pause)
53. You choose to live a healthy and happy life (7 seconds pause)
54. You overcome unhealthy habits easily (7 seconds pause)
55. You deserve an amazing life (7 seconds pause)
56. You are incredible and powerful (7 seconds pause)
57. You are positive and happier (7 seconds pause)
58. You are grateful for this change (7 seconds pause)
59. Alcohol dependency is a thing of past (7 seconds pause)

60. You relax yourself easily when you are stressed (7 seconds pause)
61. You manage stress easily (7 seconds pause)
62. You don't let anything affect your life (7 seconds pause)
63. You are living a beautiful and healthy life (7 seconds pause)
64. Life is all good and healthy now (7 seconds pause)
65. You love yourself a lot (7 seconds pause)
66. Life is beautiful (7 seconds pause)
67. You love your body (7 seconds pause)
68. Your health is most important for you (7 seconds pause)
69. You breathe fresh and clean air (7 seconds pause)
70. Your liver is getting healed (7 seconds pause)
71. Your body is your sacred place (7 seconds pause)
72. You love yourself (7 seconds pause)

73. You are full of vitality and energy (7 seconds pause)
74. You love to exercise because it makes you happy (7 seconds pause)
75. You are releasing weight effortlessly (7 seconds pause)

76. You are willing to change (7 seconds pause)
77. You let go of the past easily (7 seconds pause)
78. You are getting energetic with every passing day (7 seconds pause)
79. You pay attention to your sleep (7 seconds pause)
80. I am strong and healthy. (7 seconds pause)
81. You drink at least eight glasses of water everyday (7 seconds pause)
82. You look forward to your daily workout sessions. (7 seconds pause)
83. You listen to the signal and stop when you have eaten enough (7 seconds pause)
84. You are healthy and happy (7 seconds pause)
85. You love to exercise everyday (7 seconds pause)
86. You love to eat fruits and vegetables everyday (7 seconds pause)
87. You are becoming stronger and slimmer with every passing day (7 seconds pause)
88. When you crave sugar, you eat natural foods (7 seconds pause)
89. You are grateful for your health (7 seconds pause)

90. You are practice gratitude everyday (7 seconds pause)
91. You are open to new ways of eating (7 seconds pause)
92. You choose food that make your body stronger and healthier (7 seconds pause)
93. You chew food slowly (7 seconds pause)
94. You relish each mouthful and chew food at least 10 times (7 seconds pause)
95. You are becoming slimmer and lighter every day (7 seconds pause)
96. You love your body and mind (7 seconds pause)
97. You enjoy taking care of your body and mind (7 seconds pause)
98. You maintain sleep hygiene everyday (7 seconds pause)
99. You limit your day time naps to 30 minutes (7 seconds pause)
100. You can do it (7 seconds pause)
101. You are flexible (7 seconds pause)
102. You listen to your body (7 seconds pause)
103. You eat in moderation (7 seconds pause)
104. You eat wholesome foods (7 seconds pause)
105. You leave your past behind (7 seconds pause)

106. You feel decisive and enthusiastic (7 seconds pause)
107. You love your life (7 seconds pause)
108. You set everyday sleep and weight loss goals (7 seconds pause)
109. You take everyday actions to achieve goals (7 seconds pause)
110. You are motivated (7 seconds pause)
111. You focus on the good (7 seconds pause)
112. You are grateful (7 seconds pause)
113. You are happy (7 seconds pause)
114. You are self-aware (7 seconds pause)
115. pause)
116. .You see beauty in your body (7 seconds pause)
117. You learn new ways easily (7 seconds pause)
118. Your body is getting healed (7 seconds pause)
119. Every day you wake up you have feelings of gratitude (7 seconds pause)
120. You trust the process of life (7 seconds pause)
121. You trust yourself and trust your body (7 seconds pause)
122. You love yourself (7 seconds pause)
123. You are compassionate towards yourself (7 seconds pause)

124. You eat mindfully and enjoy every mouthful (7 seconds pause)
125. You are balanced (7 seconds pause)
126. You are competent and capable. (7 seconds pause)
127. You are worthy of love and care (7 seconds pause)
128. You give all the love and care to your own body first (7 seconds pause)
129. You choose positive thoughts (7 seconds pause)
130. You are blessed and abundant (7 seconds pause)
131. You love yourself unconditionally (7 seconds pause)
132. You are complete and whole. (7 seconds pause)
133. You are confident and courageous (7 seconds pause)
134. You forgive yourself for all the past mistakes (7 seconds pause)
135. You stay in present and are more mindful (7 seconds pause)
136. You are confident (7 seconds pause)
137. You have high self-esteem (7 seconds pause)
138. You are losing weight every day (7 seconds pause)

139. You are focused on your weight loss journey (7 seconds pause)
140. You pay attention to your food intake (7 seconds pause)
141. You love yourself unconditionally (7 seconds pause)
142. You are successful (7 seconds pause)
143. You are confident and motivated (7 seconds pause)
144. You believe in yourself (7 seconds pause)
145. You are good enough (7 seconds pause)
146. You enjoy healthy foods (7 seconds pause)
147. You do pleasurable activities everyday (7 seconds pause)
148. You are intelligent and wise (7 seconds pause)
149. You are lovable, open to receive and give love (7 seconds pause)
150. You enjoy your life and live it to the fullest (7 seconds pause)
151. You enjoy healthy food and drinks(7 seconds pause)
152. You have a beautiful relationship with food and your body (7 seconds pause)
153. You enjoy sleep and able to relax yourself easily (7 seconds pause)

154. You enjoy the process of self-hypnosis (7 seconds pause)
155. You enjoy being successful (7 seconds pause)
156. You inspire people by overcoming alcoholism (7 seconds pause)
157. You enjoy the benefits of being sober (7 seconds pause)
158. You imagine living a wonderful and long life as sober (7 seconds pause)
159. You spend more time with your family (7 seconds pause)
160. You let go of all the unhealthy habits (7 seconds pause)
161. You are success (7 seconds pause)
162. You are love (7 seconds pause)
163. You are happy (7 seconds pause)
164. You are positive (7 seconds pause)
165. You have high self-worth (7 seconds pause)
166. You enjoy living a quality life (7 seconds pause)
167. Life is wonderful (7 seconds pause)
168. You enjoy each day and live it to the fullest (7 seconds pause)
169. You are productive (7 seconds pause)
170. You are living a beautiful and healthy life now (7 seconds pause)

171. You hate the thought of drinking(7 seconds pause)
172. You enjoy every day (7 seconds pause)
173. You are a healthy and happy (7 seconds pause)
174. You are healthy and enjoy being healthy (7 seconds pause)
175. You keep your health on priority (7 seconds pause)
176. You enjoy all the benefits you see as sober (7 seconds pause)
177. You are loved (7 seconds pause) (7 seconds pause)
178. You are open to give and receive love (7 seconds pause)
179. You are in control (7 seconds pause)
180. You have high control on your habits and thoughts (7 seconds pause)
181. Your health is getting better with every passing day (7 seconds pause)
182. Your body is healing (7 seconds pause)
183. Your body is getting repaired from the alcohol (7 seconds pause)
184. You liver is getting healed(7 seconds pause)
185. You protect your inner child always (7 seconds pause)
186. You are whole and complete (7 seconds pause)

187. You love yourself unconditionally (7 seconds pause)
188. You are sober (7 seconds pause)
189. You take care of your health always (7 seconds pause)
190. You exercise regularly (7 seconds pause)
191. You eat healthy foods (7 seconds pause)
192. You enjoy the tastes of healthy foods (7 seconds pause)
193. Your sense of taste and smell is getting better with every passing day (7 seconds pause)
194. You listen to this recording regularly (7 seconds pause)
195. You are a healthy person and you inspire others (7 seconds pause)
196. You are assertive (7 seconds pause)
197. You easily say NO to alcohol (7 seconds pause)
198. You are an example for alcohol cessation (7 seconds pause)
199. You are the one who is in the driving seat of your life (7 seconds pause)
200. You are earning your right to live a sober life. (7 seconds pause)
201. You are forgiving yourself for what you did being influenced. (7 seconds pause)
202. Your life is getting unaffected by alcohol (7 seconds pause)

203. You can start finding the origin of your happiness within yourself. (7 seconds pause)
204. You are getting more powerful than your urges. (7 seconds pause)
205. You are having every reason to feel proud of yourself. (7 seconds pause)
206. You admire your physicality as well as your well-wishers. (7 seconds pause)
207. With each day, you are getting closer to the path of self-improvement. (7 seconds pause)
208. You are believing that you can get better (7 seconds pause)
209. You are becoming a better version of yourself. (7 seconds pause)
210. You are deserving of exceptional things in life (7 seconds pause)
211. You are loving the improvements in you as a person. (7 seconds pause)
212. Your loved ones love and adore you. (7 seconds pause)
213. You are becoming content with yourself (7 seconds pause)
214. You find your inner happiness with every passing day (7 seconds pause)
215. You are steadily taking charge of your own life (7 seconds pause)

216. You love and care for your body (7 seconds pause)
217. You have the power to face any hurdles that may come in your way. (7 seconds pause)
218. You have started mastering yourself to be in control. (7 seconds pause)
219. You surround yourself with supportive people (7 seconds pause)
220. You are gradually freeing yourself from your addiction to alcohol (7 seconds pause)
221. Each and every day you are getting closer to a life of being completely sober (7 seconds pause)
222. You are in charge of your life (7 seconds pause)
223. You forgive yourself for all the past mistakes done knowingly or unknowingly (7 seconds pause)
224. You have started a new life without the presence of any alcohol. (7 seconds pause)
225. With each passing day, you admire and love yourself more than before (7 seconds pause)
226. You surround yourself with healthy habits and come out as a strong individual. (7 seconds pause)

227. You have the power to reshape yourself into a more happier and peaceful person. (7 seconds pause)
228. You spend best time with the people in my life who are supportive and positive. (7 seconds pause)
229. It is natural that you are keeping yourself away from alcohol (7 seconds pause)
230. Life offers you great things and you deserve every bit of it. (7 seconds pause)
231. You are a happy and healthy individual and people start to notice it. (7 seconds pause)
232. With each passing day, your life is turning out to be better than before. (7 seconds pause)
233. You are worthy and free(7 seconds pause)
234. You have better relationships now (7 seconds pause)
235. People are finally seeing you as the one who overcomes his/her urges and habits (7 seconds pause)
236. Your body and spirit are on their way to the process of healing. (7 seconds pause)
237. Your life is eventually taking a turn for good once you set yourself free from alcohol addiction. (7 seconds pause)

238. Your choices define you and you are able to control them. (7 seconds pause)
239. You have the ability to have power over my urges to consume alcohol. (7 seconds pause)
240. You let yourself free and opt for a life without alcohol consumption. (7 seconds pause)
241. You motivate yourself to stop consuming alcohol altogether. (7 seconds pause). (7 seconds pause)
242. Your need for drinking alcohol is slowly getting released from your mind. (7 seconds pause)
243. You no longer have any impulse to drink alcohol. (7 seconds pause)
244. You don't crave for alcohol anymore as you don't find it enjoyable enough. (7 seconds pause)
245. Your life is meant to be enjoyed in many more ways other than having alcohol. (7 seconds pause)
246. You can free your life from the shackles of alcohol addiction. (7 seconds pause)
247. With each passing day, you are getting a hold on your alcohol addiction. (7 seconds pause)
248. You are getting closer to the life of sobriety with every day. (7 seconds pause)

249. You believe in yourself to quit drinking. (7 seconds pause)
250. You are bidding goodbye to your past and you are preparing to write your life's new chapter. (7 seconds pause)
251. Your relationship with people is healing along with your alcohol addiction. (7 seconds pause)
252. You deserve to lead a life full of peace and good health. (7 seconds pause)
253. You surround yourself with people who are there to love and support you. (7 seconds pause)
254. You have regained all the control in your life. (7 seconds pause)
255. One day at a time, you are starting to create your own reality. (7 seconds pause)
256. For all the choices you have made in the past, you are taking full responsibility. (7 seconds pause)
257. You are courageous and disciplined. (7 seconds pause)
258. You have gained power of self-control to relieve your life from alcohol addiction. (7 seconds pause)
259. You bring self-forgiveness into your life (7 seconds pause)
260. You become compassionate and loving towards yourself (7 seconds pause)

261. You take your commitments seriously. (7 seconds pause)
262. You are responsible. (7 seconds pause)
263. You dedicate your entire life to self-love and self-care. (7 seconds pause)
264. You learn to be more respectful toward your own body. (7 seconds pause)
265. You take care of yourself mentally, emotionally, and physically (7 seconds pause)
266. You prioritize your health more than anything. (7 seconds pause)
267. A healthy lifestyle is serving you the purpose to enjoy life even more. (7 seconds pause)
268. Every day your body is healing to become healthier. (7 seconds pause)
269. You adopt a new standard of a healthy lifestyle with this journey (7 seconds pause)
270. You enjoy the benefits of healthy habits in your life. (7 seconds pause)
271. You free yourself from everything that served you no purpose. (7 seconds pause)
272. Progression is much more important than perfection. (7 seconds pause)
273. You have the necessary faith in the process of recovery (7 seconds pause)

274. You are not going to let your past steal the thunder from your present. (7 seconds pause)
275. You are the caterpillar who thought the world was ending yet you chose to become the butterfly. (7 seconds pause)
276. The process of recovery is existing not for the ones who are in need but for the ones who want it. (7 seconds pause)
277. Recovery doesn't care about your mistakes rather it is emphasizing on lessons you are taking from your errors. (7 seconds pause)
278. Remember that growth comes from hardships and mistakes. (7 seconds pause)
279. Never go for choosing the path of excuses because it is nothing but the lies told by your own fear. (7 seconds pause)
280. You make your destiny when you allow your hardships to strengthen you. (7 seconds pause)
281. When you allow yourself to makes excuses then life makes it hard for you to excel at anything.
282. Start treat your willpower as your muscle. It gets stronger when you train it more often. (7 seconds pause)

283. All you need to do is keep going. When the time comes, everything will fall in place. (7 seconds pause)
284. Never get scared when you have to start over. Treating it like an opportunity where you can build yourself for the things you want can prove beneficial. (7 seconds pause)
285. Experience is a wonderful thing. (7 seconds pause)
286. Nobody said that it is going to be easy but it will be worth the struggle. (7 seconds pause)
287. Recovery doesn't get a day off. You keep working on it every single day for a fruitful outcome. (7 seconds pause)
288. Forgiving yourself to let go of your past mistakes. Forgiveness is another chance you can give it to yourself to start over. (7 seconds pause)
289. If you can go through the first day of quitting alcohol then you can do it for the lifetime. (7 seconds pause)
290. Your strength is not dependent on your psychical capacity rather it is arising from your power of determination. (7 seconds pause)

291. Through recovery, you are setting yourself free from your past by opening the gates of hell. (7 seconds pause)
292. Your own positive movie will be starting from the day when you have started living a sober life. (7 seconds pause)
293. Your strength is directly proportional to the things you are enduring after you're exhausted. (7 seconds pause)
294. it's time you made changes because you are the one who is holding yourself back from a beautiful life. (7 seconds pause)
295. When you strengthen yourself, you not only strengthen your body but also your confidence and self-esteem. (7 seconds pause)
296. Whenever you are denying alcohol in your life, your mind and body become more powerful. (7 seconds pause)
297. Refusing alcohol makes your mind is sharper than ever. It makes you more productive at what you do. (7 seconds pause)
298. You are well, safe, and secure (7 seconds pause)
299. You notice the positive impact of sobriety on your whole life. (7 seconds pause)
300. Everything in you life is gradually becoming better. (7 seconds pause)

301. You love the fact that you are not drinking anymore. Every aspect of life is good. (7 seconds pause)
302. You enjoy your life as a non-alcoholic. You are feeling good about yourself without the presence of alcohol in your life. (7 seconds pause)
303. Your life is great and fulfilling. (7 seconds pause)
304. You feel more than proud of your efforts to lead an alcohol-free life. (7 seconds pause)
305. Now that you have no alcohol in life, you are coming in contact with your fun and kind version of yourself. (7 seconds pause)
306. You have are finding your inner peace with every passing sober day. (7 seconds pause)
307. Being a non-drinker has made you speak more confidently and positively about your life. (7 seconds pause)
308. Your mind is getting clean and free from alcohol addiction. (7 seconds pause)
309. Now you have the will power to stay away from alcohol. (7 seconds pause)
310. With every day, you are feeling that your body is getting stronger and cleaner. (7 seconds pause)

311. You have gained control over your actions and it has helped me in making healthier lifestyle choices every day. (7 seconds pause)
312. You are strong and you are more than worthy of living a healthy life. (7 seconds pause)
313. Your body is clean and your choices have made your liver healthy again. (7 seconds pause)
314. You are entitled to keep all your organs in a stable condition. (7 seconds pause)
315. All your troubled thoughts are easily going away. Your are embracing positive habits in your life. (7 seconds pause)
316. Your heart, your nerves and your mind are getting better every day. (7 seconds pause)
317. You have opted for an alcohol-free life and it feels amazing. (7 seconds pause)
318. Now that you are away from alcohol, you will acquire a new sense of freedom in your life. (7 seconds pause)
319. With each new day, you are moving away from being alcoholic to a healthier and sober person. (7 seconds pause)
320. My nervous system and blood circulation is slowly getting better every day. (7 seconds pause)

321. Being a sober person, I no longer feel tensed in any situations. (7 seconds pause)
322. Now I can easily eliminate my urge to consume alcohol. (7 seconds pause)
323. Today I am a non-alcoholic person and I am overjoyed about it. (7 seconds pause)
324. It feels great to have clean and healthier body organs for a change. (7 seconds pause)
325. Now that I don't drink alcohol, I feel much more relaxed than ever. (7 seconds pause)
326. My body is on the recovery process in the best possible way. (7 seconds pause)
327. Every morning I wake up being satisfied with my choice of quitting alcohol. (7 seconds pause)
328. It was my choice to become a non-alcoholic being and I feel good about it. (7 seconds pause)
329. Once you choose the path of a sober person, you will start to love yourself even more. (7 seconds pause)
330. Quitting alcohol is easier than I have thought it would be. (7 seconds pause)
331. You have achieved nothing as a person who was addicted to alcohol. (7 seconds pause)

332. You can gain everything being a non-alcoholic person. (7 seconds pause)
333. Choosing a life that is not supported by alcohol is the best decision you'll ever make. (7 seconds pause)
334. Whenever I have the urge to drink, I breathe and dismiss those unhealthy thoughts. (7 seconds pause)
335. There is only exhausting hangovers and no genuine satisfaction from alcohol consumption. (7 seconds pause).
336. Time has come for you to free yourself from alcohol abuse. (7 seconds pause).
337. Now that I know myself better, I know the 'how' of quitting alcohol. (7 seconds pause).
338. You can master the art of quitting alcohol for life. (7 seconds pause).
339. You are glad that you left my days of alcohol abuse behind me. (7 seconds pause).
340. You will eventually be free from your addiction to alcohol. (7 seconds pause).
341. Meditation and long walks has made me found my inner peace. (7 seconds pause).
342. Your happiness is within you. (7 seconds pause).
343. You have to keep focusing on things that are positive in your life. (7 seconds pause).

344. Anxiety is no more a challenge and I am getting better every day. (7 seconds pause).
345. Being Calm and peaceful has become your forte. (7 seconds pause).
346. You make choices that will benefit you and your life. (7 seconds pause).
347. Once you take control of your habits, you can control of your life. (7 seconds pause).
348. Once your weakness is worn down, you will only grow with strength. (7 seconds pause).
349. Things that we repeatedly do define us and our lives. (7 seconds pause).
350. You need to maintain consistency in your life. Once you do that your habits will strengthen you. (7 seconds pause).
351. You can't stop until you reach the end of the finishing line. (7 seconds pause).
352. Attempting to live a sober life is nothing short of a marathon but I can finish it in one attempt. (7 seconds pause).
353. You can change your life by changing something you do it on a daily. (7 seconds pause).
354. You are loving the fact that your body is attaining its physical fitness. (7 seconds pause).

355. Every day your liver is healing from the alcohol abuses it faced over the past years. (7 seconds pause).
356. You get repelled over the thought of consuming even one drop of alcohol. (7 seconds pause).
357. You are happier and healthier. (7 seconds pause).
358. You are choosing your life over the sufferings that come from alcohol abuse. You are choosing a happy life over a depressed life. (7 seconds pause).
359. You are loving healthy food and you detest the presence of alcohol on your tongue. (7 seconds pause).
360. Your blood pressure isn't on higher levels anymore. All thanks to quitting alcohol. (7 seconds pause).
361. You know that you are loving yourself more than you love the toxic substance that is alcohol. (7 seconds pause).
362. You surrender yourself to the higher power (7 seconds pause).
363. You look forward to living a successful and fulfilling life (7 seconds pause).
364. You enjoy the present moment and eat healthy food (7 seconds pause).
365. You take care of your food intake and drinking habits (7 seconds pause).

366. You say NO every time you are offered drinks (7 seconds pause).
367. You know the amazing benefits of quitting alcohol (7 seconds pause).
368. You skin and your body feel amazing with every passing day (7 seconds pause).
369. It gets much easier to fall asleep (7 seconds pause).
370. You feel clean from inside (7 seconds pause).
371. People enjoy your company even more (7 seconds pause).
372. You inspire people and people look up to you (7 seconds pause).
373. You enjoy living a healthy life (7 seconds pause).
374. You love yourself fully and completely (7 seconds pause).
375. You love yourself unconditionally (7 seconds pause).
376. You like and admire yourself (7 seconds pause).
377. You are amazing (7 seconds pause).
378. You look and feel healthy (7 seconds pause).
379. People compliment you and you enjoy being healthy (7 seconds pause).
380. You look forward to living each day beautifully (7 seconds pause).

381. You are love (7 seconds pause).
382. You trust and respect yourself and your body (7 seconds pause).
383. You trust the process of life (7 seconds pause).

www.ingramcontent.com/pod-product-compliance
Lightning Source LLC
Chambersburg PA
CBHW070903080526
44589CB00013B/1163